2nd

thought

on religion

Another Face of Christ's Teachings

Pan Choul

faith books&MORE

Suwanee, Georgia

First published by Faith Books & MORE
ISBN: 978-0-9852729-1-3

Printed in the United States of America.

This book is printed on acid-free paper.

3255 Lawrenceville-Suwanee Rd.
Suite P250
Suwanee, GA 30024
publishing@faithbooksandmore.com
www.faithbooksandmore.com

Dedication

To my father and mother, Moses and Mary, and to
my wonderful sisters, Tewang and Nyadhen. In
addition to my wonderful cousin, Bayich.

Acknowledgements

Many people supported me in writing this book. My patient brother, Giw Choul, who put up with me all these years while battling illness, encouraged me to go ahead with the book and helped me in many ways. Also, I must not dismiss my great sister, Nyabana, and her husband, Pastor John, for their unwavering support spiritually and sometimes logistically. I cannot fail to remember my best friend, George Sproul. He has indeed been there for me in many ways. Thank you to my friend and author, Makur Abiar, for his recommendation of our publisher, Faith Books & MORE, that made this dream a reality. In addition, my mom and my brothers in Australia encouraged me to go with the plan of writing and helped financially. Finally, thank you to my wonderful friends, King Deng, Garang Bol, Adet, Chan, Walid, and my cousin, Guamaar.

Introduction

In our cyberspace world it is sometimes very difficult to maintain balance. With widespread violence, poverty, and crime, it is so obvious that many people miss the vitality of life, and that includes me. The reason I wrote this book is to encourage as many people as possible who are going through numerous difficulties. With disease, always with pain, sometimes comes a relief. The downward mobility and illness I have experienced compels me to write this book.

Through almost sixteen years in this country, I had reached what many called Nihilism, the state of hopelessness and despair. I read many books in the fields of philosophy and psychology. It did help a little bit, but it did not become more than a band aid to mask my condition. Until you come to the realization that you are a valuable human being to your creator, you will never discover the true meaning of life. It is simply a self-discovery.

It has been said that God has a plan for each individual, but sometimes we keep turning around at the same place without a clue of what that plan might be. To some it comes early in time; to others it could be a lifetime journey. Discovering that plan in your life could be when you are in the lowest stage of your life. We tend to blame our shortcoming on others, government or disease. In fact, the downward spiral could be the exact place God wants us to be in order to discover what our mission is.

Love and peace are all around us, but sometimes we fail to notice them because we are pessimistically primed. Our self-image is affected. All of life is affected. Then we lose faith in ourselves, our neighbors, even God. You may be struggling because you have not recognized God's plan, his mission, for you. This book came as I reflected on the Bible in combination with self-help books proven to lift or partially boost the self-esteem.

Self-help books will not take you to a magic world where there is no suffering. They will not erase the hurting self-image. But with discovery of our mission or God's plan to our lives, these resources help us recover.

When diagnosed with schizophrenia fourteen years ago, I thought it was my end. But sometimes whatever you go through can be a gift in disguise. I love writing, and I believe this is what God wants me to do. In addition, I hope to help those who might be undergoing tragedies understand that what seems to be holding you back could be just what you need to get ahead.

TABLE OF CONTENTS

Love could mean sacrificing our assets or even the most important thing we have on behalf of those we love.
Pan Choul

1

Loving God

"Know then that the Lord your God is God, the faithful God. He keeps His promise and shows His loving-kindness to those who love Him and keep His laws, even to a thousand family groups in the future" (Deuteronomy 7:9 NLV).

The world we live in is a terrible place. With the spread of violence, hatred, and crime, it seems as if God is not in control of the kingdom of men. Humankind think that God is not in control or that he is not interested in human suffering, but this is not true at all. God is a loving God and at the same time he is the God of justice. Therefore, His love does not compromise His justice.

2 God also is the God of mercy. "The Lord, the Lord, the compassionate and gracious God, slow to anger, abounding in love and faithfulness, maintaining love to thousands, and forgiving wickedness, rebellion and sin. Yet he does not leave the guilty unpunished; he punishes the children and their children for the sin of the parents to the third and the fourth generation" (Exodus 34:6-7 NIV).

Sometimes when we lose our way and sink to the bottom of life we give up, thinking and concluding that God has already given up on us, that he simply does not care about what we are going through. Therefore, we start sinning much more. What I am trying to say is that sometimes we are responsible for what is happening in our lives and certainly we contribute to some of the things we go through. But through my reading of the Bible, I notice that some people were destroyed because of the wrong done by people before them. Their punishment came as a fulfillment of what God said would take place. We know that God is a just God and he does not lie. Therefore, whatever he said through the mouths of his prophets always took place, whether instantly or later, according to his will.

God punishes any sin we commit. If we do not repent and seek God's forgiveness, we pay dearly. Our heavenly father said that He loves those who love Him. We also know that the greatest commandment is to love God with all our hearts, souls, minds, and spirits, and to love our neighbors as ourselves. When we do this, we show our love for God, and he then reveals himself to us. "I love those who love me, and those who look for me with much desire will find me" (Proverbs 8:17 NIV).

We witnessed how God talked face to face with Moses, and how he led the children of Israel out of Egypt to the promise land with a strong hand. We also witnessed how the children of Israel, when they were hungry, thirsty, or heard rumors of attacks against them from foreign kings, many times turned their backs on God by doubting God's deliverance. The children of Israel are not the only ones lacking faith **3** in God. In just the same way, Christians today doubt God sometimes when things happen to us such as being fired from work or when someone we love gets sick or dies. It is these types of tragedies that cause us to turn away from God.

Our God is a very mighty God. He is not a man to feel sorry for whatever he does. We saw God grieved during Noah's time, but he was grieved by mankind's actions, not his own. And he did not grieve after his justice was complete (Genesis 6:5). The Lord saw that man's wickedness on the earth had become great and that every inclination of the thoughts of his heart was evil all the time. The Lord was grieved that he had made man on the earth, and His heart was filled with pain.

I would like to shed a little light on this issue, the grief of God. It always compels Him to justice and salvation. That is the difference between God and man. When man grieves, his grievances work death and surrender to whatever caused the grievances. However, when God grieves, he changes things and the changes result in moving from worse to better. We have seen how God changes things since the creation and even in our recent days. Our God is perfect and he is a working God. When we look for him with desire, we will find him just as he promised.

Our heavenly father still talks to us through his teachings. In old times, God addressed the children of Israel himself while they stood away from Mount Sinai. Then because of their unfaithfulness, God stopped talking to Israel, but he still talked with his prophets. Whenever God wanted to do something, he sent the prophet King and directed him about what God wanted to done. Also in our day, God still talks to us if we follow his teachings and do them. Jesus said in John 14:21, "The one who loves me is the one who has my teaching and obeys it. My father will love whoever loves me. I will love him and will show myself to him." Jesus is the primary example for us; he never does anything without his father's acceptance. He obeys him perfectly even to the death on the cross. Therefore, his father made his name above all others. Every knee will bow before him and every tongue will confess that he is Lord. God also promised blessing and riches to those who love him and he fills their storehouses (Proverbs 8:21). Those who come to realize that God is the creator of earth and Heaven and the supplier of them give their lives to him and also love him so much. By doing that, God enriches and fills them.

In addition to that, God loves Jesus Christ so much that he sent him to the world to show us and reveal to us the love of God so that we may experience it as Jesus experienced it and became one with his father (John 17:26). When we experience this love, it changes us and will make us perfect. This love will also unite us as one. Through this unity, the world will know that our savior has been sent by the father. Our heavenly father sent his only begotten son to redeem us. This shows us that God loves us.

Our heavenly father takes care of those he loves, but sinners hate God.

Therefore, they are destroyed (Psalm 145:20). The Bible states we have to ask God for loving favor. God loves Christ with a love that never gets weak. But we know that sometimes we feel our love for God sour and things of Satan come and weaken that love. Therefore we have to ask God constantly to strengthen our love and make it strong even when we go through trouble. If our love remains strong, we rest assured that He will bring us out of trouble and set us safe in high places. When we love him, we reflect our knowledge of him. Those who hate do not know God because God is love.

There is a wonderful thing the eye has never seen, no ear has ever heard, no mind has ever thought of. That is what God has made ready for those who love Him. Some people reject and disobey the laws of God. However, he is still telling us today to love the Lord our God and work for Him with all our hearts and souls. In addition, if we do just that he will give rain for our land at the right times, the early and the late rains, so we may gather grain, new wine, and oil. He will give grass in the fields for our cattle, and we will eat and be filled.

Poverty in our society happens because people reject the name of God. People feel uncomfortable if the name of God is even mentioned in their business meetings. Many businesses fail because the owners do not love or recognize God as the source of their success. There are shortages of food and life's necessities because men want to replace the source of life with man's intellectual machinery and mammon to sustain it. Man has forgotten that knowledge is not enough. Only God is the supplier of this universe. He created man and only he is capable of maintaining life and existence. Man replacing God's plan with his own is the source of inflation, poverty, and even death in the world.

2

Why Poverty

According to many sources and personal experiences, poverty is one strategy the devil uses to destroy believers. Most of the prison population comes from broken homes. I do not assert that all of those in prison came from unfortunate situations. But Satan's primary goal is to destroy homes then to extend his attacks to the church, the community, and finally, the nation. Satan's prime target is the family. The problem of divorce contributes vastly to poverty. It begets teen pregnancy, homelessness, and rebellion against law and authority. Children growing up without parental role-modeling, and I mean spiritual role-modeling, is what opens the door to rebellion and selfish living. Selfish life leads to hatred toward God and man. It is only through God that we can learn how to escape poverty. God is the one who gives and takes. Without faith in God, man cannot escape when the devil lays a hand on him. When you are raised in a broken home or a dysfunctional family, if you do not believe and obey God's laws, it will be hard for you to escape the devil's traps against you or your family.

We Christians were advised by the Apostle Paul that doing our best to live a quiet life and performing our work well will cause us to be respected by those who are not Christians. We will not be in need or looking for others to help us. Laziness is the chief reason for poverty. If we love God with hearts full of love, God will drive laziness away and we will do our work as if we are doing it for the Lord.

The Bible states that the soul of the lazy person has strong desires and gets nothing, but the soul of the one who does his best gets more than he needs. The lazy person desires many things but always fails to achieve them. In order for us to get something, we have to do the work. Thievery is rampant because people reject work. They want to get something that they did not work for. However, thievery could be stopped if the person were willing to pay the price. Unfortunately, it does not occur to a thief that the thing he has stolen exists because someone worked for it.

I believe that everyone is born with all dignities and nobilities inside him, resources that enable him to contribute to his fellow man; for example, intellect, honor, and nobility. He might even be born with abilities to create wealth so that he can share it with those who don't have it. However, if he rejects God and his laws, the enemy blinds him to the truth.

God revealed himself perfectly in the Bible; revealed his power, character, love, faithfulness, justice, mercy, etc. David said it in Psalms: "The fear of God is the beginning of wisdom" (Psalm 111:10 NIV). If we are willing to learn his word from cover to cover we will come to unfold the knowledge of God. God is always true to abide by his laws. We exist because of his mercy and love. In addition, if we always come to him with repentant hearts he can lead us constantly. Rather, man rejected the rule of God. The people asked for a King while God was the only faithful King they needed.

Man is still facing a lot of trouble today. Jesus Christ our Savior came to earth to die for our sins and paid the full price for our redemption, but man was not satisfied by his death on a cross. People still nail the savior to the cross by the work of sin in order to escape poverty. To bring riches, you must work hard with all you might as for the Lord. Those who yearn to be rich without work set themselves up for failure.

Some people fake work. There is a difference between fake work and overcapacity work. If the work is too heavy for you, it is right to be honest with your employer and ask for help. If the employer is honest and fears God, he will work with you. However, if the employer does not work with you in this matter then maybe this is not what God wants you to be doing. In any place of work there are a variety of roles. If you are not able to do great in a certain role, ask your manager for the best way to do it. But if you tried and it did not work out, maybe ask for a different role. If you are not faking it, they will likely find you a different role for you. If this does not work out it may be time to get out and find something else that fits your abilities.

There is another fact that can contribute directly to poverty: addiction to drugs and alcohol. Addiction affects the human brain and the person's ability to make decisions. Some people find themselves not wanted at their jobs because they are incapable of doing the task. But many lose their jobs simply because of miscommunication with their bosses. They may fail to submit to the existing culture or set of rules the employer requires. Most of these errors are rebellion against the employer's job code. Addiction is a pivotal ailment that contributes to this condition. I am not suggesting that you have to sit idle due to addiction. Rather, identify those demons that would drag you down to poverty. A lot of nonprofit organizations in this country can help you reduce addiction and be loosed from it.

In addition to physical poverty, addiction is the backbone of spiritual poverty. Many people withdraw from their churches because they think believers have undermined them. This can be partially true. But one thing the addict should know is that not all people of churches have the same measure of faith.

The apostle Paul mentioned in 2 Thessalonians 3:10-12 that there were Thessalonians who did not want to work. They spent their time trying to see what others were doing. Paul himself, being a traveling preacher, did not rely on believers to supply his needs. Even as a prisoner in Rome, Paul continued to work to supply his needs by his own hands. That is a perfect example to the church today.

I am not intending to judge preachers who rely on their flocks for their salaries. It is right for the farmer to benefit from the field and the preacher has the same role in the house of the Lord as the Levites in the old days. Priests who were Levites—indeed, the whole tribe of Levi—were to have no allotment or inheritance. They were to live on the offerings made to the Lord as their inheritance. "They shall have no inheritance among their fellow Israelites; the Lord is their inheritance, as he promised them" (Deuteronomy 18:2 NIV). However, for the sake of flexibility and freedom, Paul decided not to be deprived of his pride. He continued to work in order to sustain his needs.

I have heard that some preachers have been turned away from the truth and the word of God by those who wanted to hear what pleased them. If you're a preacher and it happens that you are pleasing man and not God, you're no longer true to the faith. The pastor must obey God more than man. If it happens that the roles are reversed, you are no longer serving God.

Those in the church who are idle, if they are in good health, should seek advice to work so they will be able to eat their own food. The Bible reveals that those who work their land will have more than enough food, but those who waste their time will become poor. Whether you are a businessperson, teacher, politician, carpenter, fisherman, scientist, sportsman, preacher, or soldier, if you don't strive in your existing field you will not succeed and will lack in provision. If you are a teacher, be a hard-working teacher. If you are a doctor, work hard in your craft. By so doing you will have enough to sustain yourself and your family.

Some people are gifted in certain crafts or fields but they do not use them and they remain in poverty. Mismanagement and wrongdoing also cause gifted people to fail to succeed and stay in poverty. In fact,

God gives talents but when you fail to shift those talents in the right direction they will not do you any good. For example, someone might be gifted in science, but is too lazy to discover new ideas or refuses to investigate the possibilities of his surroundings and opportunities God has endowed him with in his daily life. Darwin, Newton, Abbert, Addison, and Freud were able to use their talents to contribute to the human family. God put all these elements around us so we could benefit from them and contribute to the betterment of mankind. All these technological discoveries are intended to draw us closer to our creator not take us further from him.

12 We know that despite the triumph of man, his discoveries, exploration of the heavens—Mars, the moon—these are only fractions of the knowledge of God. Man, with all his advances in technology, thinks he might be close to the mind of God. We cannot know the mind of God. God's mind is infinite. We only know His characteristics, but he knows our minds.

We know the laws of God, and He does not contradict himself. We cannot confine him to his laws. Only he can make laws and change them. As He states, "'My thoughts are not your thoughts, neither are your ways my ways,' declares the LORD" (Isaiah 55:8 NIV). All man's advances and discoveries cannot save himself or bring the dead back to life. Only God can do that. As we have seen, Jesus gave his life on the cross and took it up again. We make mistakes when we even write a book and title it, The Mind of God. This is insulting to our heavenly father who does everything according to his pleasure. He created man in his own image and man chose not to abide by his laws. However, God did not abandon man completely. Rather, he punishes man as a father would punish his child who rebels against his authority. Our heavenly father sent his son Jesus to be the redeemer of the world and those who believe in Him shall never die, but have eternal life. However, calling on the name of the Lord alone will not guarantee us his kingdom. We also have to do the will of God in order to enter the Kingdom of God.

Those who want to escape poverty must work hard and not obsess with too much sleep. Sleep is an element of nourishment and vibration. When we have a good sleep our memory is enhanced and our thoughts are fresh. Either too little sleep or too much will bring us to poverty in the end.

Less sleep for a long period can affect our ability to make right decisions, whether at work or home. It can even cause stress-related illnesses such as depression and related mental illnesses. God designed the night so that people could rest for a certain period and **13** be renewed to face the load of the next day. Charged with enough strength, we can be happy, but work without strength makes a person miserable. Exhaustion prevents us from enjoying our work. Rather, it becomes a burden we must bear. God wants us to be happy in what we are doing for him.

The hardest job was the one our savior did here on earth, the work of salvation. Jesus Christ worked here and conducted his father's business with all his heart. He did not complain, faint, or quit when the time came for his crucifixion. Our Savior was willing to pay the full price for our salvation and he completed the work. Those who believe in him shall never die, but will have eternal life. Therefore, our Savior is the greatest example of relationships between employers and employees. Jesus Christ maintained a great relationship with those he chose as his disciples. He rebuked them when they sinned, but in a loving manner. He also complimented them when they got the job done and done right. Our savior, who is God in the flesh, third person in the Godhead, was able to fulfill both roles of employer and employee. Even this earth was created through him and he is the image of the invisible God doing his father's will perfectly.

Oversleep is one of the reasons that people lose their jobs. It is not in the interest of most employers when employees miss work or are late because they overslept. It might be taken lightly the first time, but if he allows it to continue I do not think that is a sign of a good employer. Therefore, the book of Proverbs advises, "Do not love sleep or you will become poor. Open your eyes, and your will be filled with food" (Proverbs 20:13 NLV). The Bible reveals in the book of Proverbs that the path of the faithful is a good road.

Being lazy is a sign of unfaithfulness. If we remain unfaithful to our employers or in our work, we create setbacks, difficulties, or various other problems. The Mormon believes that work is a foundation of the church. Paul mentions in his letters that if the Christian is unfaithful in providing for his family through his own specialty, he is worse than an unbeliever. The ability and willingness to care for your own is a result of faith.

When Jesus Christ was on this earth he never sent away anyone in need of physical help, deliverance from disease, or food. Our savior provided all human needs. It is not enough for us to provide for the spiritual needs of our family and friends. We have to extend a helping hand in terms of material needs as well because, as the Bible said, what is the good of a Christian telling those who come to him for help to go and be warm without extending assistance while waiting on God to provide for him? Your small charity is part of God's plan to sustain them and delivery them from that problem. Allowing laziness in our daily lives develops unfaithfulness and unfaithfulness unbalances our personal and professional lives.

God is a just God. Whatever he reveals in his word is true and perfect. Unfaithfulness to our employers will lay thorns in our way. We will receive what we give. If we give bad complements to our co-workers then that is exactly what we will get. If we choose to deal unrespectable or harshly with our co-workers or bosses we should not expect a different outcome.

Once I was working for Compax Plastics, a company that makes hygiene products. It happened that I established a strong relationship with my boss. He trusted me and often shared with me even personal matters concerning other employees. On a certain day, he shared with me an incident that took place with one of the employees who always treated him with disrespect. That made him furious. Peter (not his real name) intimidated a fellow employee and treated him exactly the way he did. My boss related this story to me and told me what he should expect. He crossed boundaries therefore I gave him what he asked for. I mention this incident because some people forget that we are all in debt to someone else. Your boss is accountable to the owner of the company, and the owner himself is accountable to the law and to God.

I want this clearly out in the open. If you are a person who fears God and you expect blessings from God, open your ear to what God stated in his word. God is not a man that he should lie. Every word of God is true. "Slaves, obey your earthly masters with respect and fear, and with sincerity of heart, just as would obey Christ. Obey them not only to win their favor when their eye is on you, but as slaves of Christ, doing the will of God from your heart. Serve wholeheartedly, as if you were serving the Lord, not people, because you know that the lord will reward each one for whatever good they do, whether they are slave or free. And masters, treat your slaves in the same way. Do not threaten them, since you know that he who is both their Master and yours is in heaven, and there is no favoritism with him" (Ephesians 6:5-9 NIV).

One thing every employee should realize is that he and the employer are both accountable to God and he is master over them all. The employee should respect and honor the employer as he is doing it for the Lord and the employer should not threaten or practice favoritism between the employees knowing that he is accountable to God who gives and takes. It is your duty to do the right thing even though there is no one watching you. Our heavenly father is always watching and rewards each of us according to our work.

Work that has been effectively planned is most productive. Some employers are only interested in fast work and productivity, but large production does not always guarantee satisfaction or wealth. It may even lead to failure. God is interested in a plan. Most of the Books I read about technological advancement refer to Japan's emphasis on quality of the product not quantity. That is why Japanese cars are far more desirable even in the United States, the leading technological country in the world.

God created man in his own image; therefore, man holds inside him the wisdom and knowledge to get things done. The first teacher and engineer was God himself. It did not take God a lot of study or research to create the universe. He is the master and nothing surpasses his might and power. God created the earth by his word. He said it and it was done.

God was the instructor to Israel from their exodus from Egypt to the Promised Land. He was the one who instructed them to build the temple. He gave them his wisdom and spirit to make things; whether farming or an invention, God was the power behind it. But the children of Israel refused to listen to God's voice. Rather than using their God-given knowledge, we see that they made a golden calf to worship. That displeased God and he slew many of them. "When the people saw that Moses was so long in coming down from the mountain, they gathered around Aaron and said, 'Come, make us gods who will before us. As for this fellow Moses who brought us

up out of Egypt, we don't know what has happened to him'"
(Exodus 32:1-2 NIV).

The Bible states that knowledge generates pride and success in
technological discoveries deceives man and makes him think he is in
charge. Man's power always destroys because it is filled with
selfishness and pride. Search for power is what made the devil.
Lucifer was motivated by the same evil intention that drives man
today. Power itself does not guarantee safety or peace if it is acquired
through evil acts. Power that is motivated by selfishness and greed
always destroys those who have it. Worldly power always demolishes
and diminishes.

17

We have witnessed how nations that were once powerful became
weak; for example, Babylon, Greece, Medio Persia, and the Roman
Empire. Power itself could shift if it is misused. In the Bible, I have
learned about kingdoms mightier with weaponry and technological
might than their counterparts that fell simply because they
undermined the rule of God over them. They changed the laws of
God and boasted in their false pride, which caused God to root
them out of existence.

3

Money

God wants us to prosper and live peacefully on this earth before we join him in heaven. If we recognize God in our daily and professional lives, it will be well with us. Proverbs 27:23 (NLV) reads: "Know well how your flocks are doing, and keep your mind on your cattle." How many businesses today are motivated by profits and neglect the employee? As clear in the word of God, effective leadership and management are part of God's plan. Without effective leadership or management, many businesses lose profits. If you want to be successful in any given job, first it is critical to learn how to manage yourself. If you trust God with all your heart, mind, and soul, God promised, "The Lord will open for you His good store-house, the heavens. He will give rain to your land at the right time. He will bring good to all the work you do. You will give to many nations. But you will not use anything that belongs to them" (Deuteronomy 28:12 NLV). When you work faithfully with your employer God promises you will be paid for your work. The Bible reveals: "All the work he began in the house of God, obeying the laws and looking to his God, he did with all his heart and all went will for him" (2 Chronicles 31:21 NLV). Therefore, if all work begins in the house of God no matter what we doing, we are doing it for God. I do not mean God wants anything from man except his heart. Nothing in the world we can do would impress God except our hearts, mind, and souls. We cannot give anything to God because he is the one who gives and takes.

The only food that will satisfy man's soul is to do the will of the father. Jesus, our savior, said it clearly: "My food is to do what God wants me to do and finish his work," (John 4:34 NLV), and Christ did finish the work of his father when he died on the cross. We do not have any excuse if we reject God's plan for us.

Money is a very confusing topic. Some believers, when they come to Christianity, do not explore the Bible concerning the topic of money. The Bible has a clear vision about how we should perceive money. Some scriptures describe money as a tool or a means for our own service. Some even go so far as to say lack of money is accompanied by despair and unhappiness while a lot of money brings happiness and opportunities. However, let us follow closely what Jesus said to the people on the mountain. "No one can serve two masters. Either you will hate the one and love the other, or you will be devoted to the one and despise the other. You cannot serve both God and money" (Matthew 6:24 NIV).

Someone might well ask, "Pan, you talk about the importance of work and deliverance from poverty; how can one combat poverty without money?" That is exactly what I am trying to say. Money **21** cannot deliver you from poverty. Only God himself can do that because those whose goal is chasing money as their master are still in the yolk of slavery. Love of money is worshipping a false God. Money is an idol because it does not have a spirit in itself. Money does not feel or smell. Only God gives victory and deliverance. Those who love money will not be satisfied by it. Money does not have life in itself. Those who lay their trust upon mammon will learn that it will fail them. Our savior made it clear that we have only one master and he is God.

God is the source of everything. He is the source of life and wealth. There is a popular phrase in the Bible: "The love of money is the root of all-evil..." (I Timothy 6:10 KJV). The phrase is very clear. It does not say money is evil. Rather, it is says the love of money is the root of evil. There is nothing wrong with having money, but there is something wrong with loving it. The verse continues, "...Some people, eager for money, have wandered from the faith and pierced themselves with many griefs" (1 Timothy 6:10 NIV).

Christians should not pursue money because that will hurt their faith. We should not put our faith in anything besides God. He is the only one who can deliver us from poverty. "Do not work hard to be rich. Stop trying to get things for yourself. When you set your eyes upon it, it is gone. For sure, riches make themselves wings like an eagle that flies toward the heavens" (Proverb 23:4-5 NLV).

Money should not be the primary motivation for doing work. Rather, work should be the act of honoring God. We should glorify God with our work. This does not mean we should continue working even though the employer no longer pays our wages. We should receive an honest paycheck for the hours put in. It means God is not pleased when we cheat or con, because he is a just and honest God.

These days there are a lot of self-help books talking about financial independence. Money itself is not independent. How could money free you from bondage? A person who totally forgets God in search of mammon will find terrible problems. People think they could break free of financial worries if they just had enough money. This is not true. Money might be lost through inflation, death, mismanagement, or theft. The only true financial independence is found through faith in God.

Many people are in debt and will never break free by pursuing wealth because only God is able to free them from that degrading pit. Jesus said if you know the truth, the truth will set you free. If you are in debt, I advise you to turn to God for deliverance. I am not saying to ignore the suggestions of those who apply certain principles to help you experience financial freedom, but you should first look to God's laws. They will set you free eternally.

Jesus said to the multitude on the Sermon of the Mount, "Do not store up for yourselves treasures on earth, where moth and rust destroy, and where thieves break in and steal. But store up for yourselves treasures in heaven, where moth and rust do not destroy, and where thieves do not break in and steal. For where your treasure is, there your heart will be also" (Matthew 6:19-21 NIV). According to this verse, there is clearly nothing wrong with acquiring wealth. Jesus does not condemn those who pursue wealth, but rather he is concerned about what they treasure. If your storehouse is on this earth you are wasting your time and energy. If your goal is to acquire wealth for the sake of power and personal glory and not for furthering the kingdom of God, you are deceiving yourself, because those who are acquiring wealth to feed the pleasures of their hearts will no longer be right with God. When our goal is to further the work of God and our love for Him, riches or wealth will not twist us. **23** Some people cheat, dictate, steal, or even kill for the sake of riches. This strategy for acquiring wealth is an abomination in the sight of God. Some people might do it intentionally because they do not know God; for example, the case of the tax collector, Zacchaeus. When he came to know Jesus Christ, Zacchaeus realized his wrongdoings and decided to repay those whom he had harmed and robbed. I believe God will forgive those who repent of their wrongdoing.

The word of God clearly states that the few things the man has who is right with God are better than the riches of sinful men. We should not envy those who have more than we do because when we are right with God he is pleased with us even when we have little. People make mistakes. Some religious leaders wrongly assume that being poor is a sign of something wrong in a person's relationship with God. In the Sermon on the Mount, Jesus said, "Blessed are the poor in spirit, for theirs is the kingdom of Heaven" (Matthew 5:3 NIV). Once I came across an article written by a Christian author about this topic. He mentioned that the poor in spirit are not necessarily poor in worldly materials. I totally disagree. Jesus was not referring to a humble spirit because if that were what he meant the person would be meek, and Jesus said in Matthew 5:7 (KJV), "Blessed are the meek, for they shall inherit the earth." In order to shed light clearly on this topic, God related to us in the book of Luke the story of a rich man and a beggar named Lazarus. It goes like this.

There was a rich man who was dressed in purple and fine linen and lived in luxury every day. At his gate was laid a beggar named Lazarus, covered with sores and longing to eat what fell from the rich man's table. Even the dogs came and licked his sores. The time came when the beggar died and the angels carried him to Abraham's side. The rich man also died and was buried. In Hades, where he was in torment, he looked up and saw Abraham far away, with Lazarus by his side.

So he called to him, "Father Abraham, have pity on me and send Lazarus to dip the tip of his finger in water and cool my tongue, because I am in agony in this fire."

But Abraham replied, "Son, remember that in your lifetime you received your good things, while Lazarus received bad things, but now he is comforted here and you are in agony. And besides all this, between us and you a great chasm has been set in place, so that those who want to go from here to you cannot, nor can anyone cross over from there to us."

He answered, "Then I beg you, father, send Lazarus to my family, for I have five brothers. Let him warn them, so that they will not also come to this place of torment."

Abraham replied, "They have Moses and the Prophets; let them listen to them."

"No, father Abraham," he said, "but if someone from the dead goes to them, they will repent."

He said to him, "If they will not listen to Moses and the Prophets, they will not be convinced even if someone rises from the dead" (Luke 16:19-31 NIV).

This story shows clearly that when we refuse to share our wealth with the poor or needy, we will be judged for this. But how would the rich man know he was accountable to the needy?

I read a self-help book years back and the author mentioned that no matter how good we are doing there is someone who is doing even **25** better or no matter how bad we are doing there is someone who is even worse.

When I was growing up back in Sudan, though we were not poor, we were not doing that well. But it did not ever cross my mind once that we were further down on the economic ladder than some others. At the same time, there were many people doing worse than we were but I did not know it until much later after I was released from jail.

When I came to this community I checked myself into a rescue mission for alcohol treatment. I came to realize that even though I was a refugee with a low-paying job from one of the most improvised countries in the world I was doing better than many people struggling with addictions without a job or a place to live though they lived in one of the wealthiest countries in the world. Through the treatment program, I revived my spiritual walk with the Lord and developed the habit of reading once again. In fact, I had developed a love of reading in my earliest years.

In Sudan, in March of 1993, upon completing high school and earning my diploma, it happened that I came to know Christ in a town called Shendi in the north of Sudan. I had departed from Khartoum, the capital of Sudan, where we were living at the time, and went to live with my sister. Her husband was head of the Shendi hospital.

Before I came to Shendi, I met a young man who was part of the youth group called (YCF) Young Christian Fellowship. Our family was well-known and popular in the community due to our background, which I am not interested in sharing with you at this time. The young man found his way to our home. I was in the living room studying mathematics, my favorite subject. He began to speak with me. He told me he could see I was not happy and that I was burdened. For the sake of my pride and dignity, I snapped back at him. I told him I was just fine and I was not burdened with anything. But inside, I knew I was lying though I would never admit that. I was scared and confused.

Devoid of Christ, many people know there is something wrong even though they may not acknowledge it at the time. They notice born-again believers and know inside something is not right.

After we talked a little bit he asked me to pray and ask Jesus to come into my life. I repeated the words after him without knowing what that was supposed to mean. The next day he left the city.

In Shendi (North Sudan), I met a kid who was about to turn sixteen years old. I was nineteen at the time. He asked me to accompany him to church and I said sure. There were small churches not far from my home. As we walked, we came to the church and sat down. Young men and kids were sharing their spiritual experiences about how Christ had changed their lives. The stories fascinated me. One particular kid interested me very much. I was moved by his courage and the way he conducted himself, sang hymns, and talked in tongues. I said to myself, "I want to know more about Christ, the one who changed this boy from the way he was.

Fortunately, those kids were part of the YCF, Young Christian Fellowship Group, young people from different Christian denominations who had accepted Christ as their Lord and Savior and formed this mission organization to strengthen their home churches. At the time, they brought in order with them. They had religious tracts and spiritual books to sell for a small fee. This enabled them to further the mission work.

27

I picked up an Arabic translation, entitled "Salvation," and then I went home. I started reading a few chapters of the book every day. After a few days, I came to know Christ and his work of salvation and redemption. At the same time, I felt different. The way I used to perceive God changed even though I was a Christian and had been going to church every Sunday with my family. I did not know you could have a personal relationship with God and Christ. I did not know you could live in God and his guidance every day. I did not know the consequences of my sins. I knew that disobeying God was wrong but I did not know the consequence of sin. I knew that committing adultery was a sin, as in with a married woman, but I did not know that committing adultery with any woman you were not married to was a sin. I knew that using violence against an innocent person was a sin, but I did not know even being angry with your brother was the same as assaulting or murdering them.

One day I walked to the bathroom. Instead of taking a bath, I knelt down and asked God to come into my life. From that moment when I accepted Jesus as my Lord and Savior, I felt free. From that moment on, I found myself happy and joyful. I even gained some weight.

Before I came to know the Lord I had been tiny and very skinny. I was not naturally skinny. I was that way because I was burdened down with a heavy yoke of sin. I used to be stressed all the time, which compelled me to keep myself busy solving math problems to get some relief.

After I went back to Khartoum where my family was living, I decided to collect books for myself. There was a man who lived a few blocks from us who was into electronics. Apparently, he didn't have enough capital to open a shop so he did all his work in his backyard. Whenever there was a problem with my stereo, I would run it down to him and he would fix it for a small amount of money. When I decided to collect books, I needed to acquire a bookshelf to keep my books on after I finished reading them. I never got rid of any of my books. I kept them all. So I went to my neighbor to ask him if he could make me a bookshelf. He agreed. We settled on a price and the next day I picked up my new bookshelf.

In a few days, I came upon a small book titled Angels by an evangelist named Billy Graham. It was an Arabic translation because that was the only language I was proficient in at the time. Through this publication, Mr. Graham taught me a lot about the role of angels on behalf of believers. The book strongly strengthened my faith in God. To be frank, it dragged the fear of death out of my life and helped me a lot in my journey, which led me to America.

On my journey, I faced many deadly incidents. I could have been badly hurt or even killed during some of these situations. However, because I was informed beforehand about the role of angels on behalf of believers, I was secure in God's might and protection. When we doubt the ability of God to protect us in times of trouble, we commit sin against God and hurt ourselves in the process. When God sends a man to work for him, he sends an angel before him.

When God asks you to do something, if you obey his voice and trust him, he guarantees your success.

The reason I relate my story here is not to claim that I have walked perfectly with God, because I have not. I do not know why I went back to my life of sin after I accepted Jesus Christ as my Lord. I still do not understand why I became a wine drinker. I have asked myself that question several times and I have discovered there is a difference between accepting Jesus Christ as Lord and as Savior of your life. Those who accept Jesus as Lord and Savior must understand what Jesus wants to save them from. After coming to know Jesus, I realized I did not understand what those words meant.

29

It is popular today for preachers to invite people to the altar, and introduce them to Christ, but what people really need is not an introduction to Christ, but to find Christ. The person must know that all people have sinned and fallen short of the glory of God (Romans 3:23). He needs to believe that he has personally sinned and fallen short of God's glory. In addition, he needs to know that the wages of sin is death, but the gift of God is eternal life in Christ Jesus our Lord (Romans 6:23). He needs to believe that because accepting the Lord without a clear understanding will not make a person a strong believer but will make him self-righteous.

I recall when I was new in Christian faith I would find myself acting superior to those who had been delivered from sexual sins because when I accepted Christ I was living an honorable life according to earthly standards. At that time, I was not a wine drinker, had never dated a woman, and had a logical, academic intellect. I had been a top student in my class a couple of times and these abilities according to earthly measures were regarded with honor and admiration.

Jesus Christ shared the story of the woman who massaged his feet with fine oil. Those with him asked why this act of love would be measured differently toward God and the Savior versus others. Here's what happened.

When one of the Pharisees invited Jesus to have dinner with him, he went to the Pharisee's house and reclined at the table. A woman in that town who lived a sinful life learned that Jesus was eating at the Pharisee's house, so she came there with an alabaster jar of perfume. As she stood behind him at his feet weeping, she begun to wet his feet with her tears. Then she wiped them with her hair, kissed them and poured perfume on them.

When the Pharisee who had invited him saw this, he said to himself, "If this man were a prophet, he would know who is touching him and what kind of woman she is—that she is a sinner."

Jesus answered him, "Simon, I have something to tell you."

"Tell me, teacher," he said.

"Two people owed money to a certain moneylender. One owed him five hundred denarii, and the other fifty. Neither of them had the money to pay him back, so he forgave the debts of both. Now which of them will love him more?"

Simon replied, "I suppose the one who had the bigger debt forgiven."

"You have judged correctly," Jesus said. Then he turned toward the woman and said to Simon, "Do you see this woman? I came into your house. You did not give me any water for my feet, but she wet my feet with her tears and wiped them with her hair. You did not give me a kiss, but this woman, from the time I entered, has not stopped kissing my feet. You did not put oil on my head, but she has poured perfume on my feet. Therefore, I tell you, her many sins have been forgiven—as her great love has shown. But whoever has been forgiven little loves little." Then Jesus said to her, "Your sins are forgiven" (Luke 7:36-49 NIV).

This story reveals that believers will love God differently. Those who realize that their many sins are forgiven will love more. Believers must realize that even one sin is huge in the sight of God. If we do not acknowledge that, we will find it difficult to fully love God. Jesus said in John 14:21 (NLV), "The one who loves Me is the one who has My teaching and obeys it. My father will love whoever loves Me. I will love him and show Myself to him."

From my study of the book of Job, I have come to understand some things about God. "In the land of Uz there lived a man whose name was Job. This man was blameless and upright; he feared God and shunned evil" (Job 1:1 NIV). Because Job feared God and shunned evil, his fear of God even compelled him to pray for his children early in the morning. He thought, "Perhaps my children have sinned and cursed God in their hearts." This was Job's regular custom.

If we follow the scenario closely, we find that it was not the devil that brought up the name of Job. God brought Job to the devil's attention. I do not understand why God talked to the devil and made a deal with him. As well as the rest of the angels, God created him. We know that Lucifer was created by God as one of his angels. He was referred to as a morning star. "How you have fallen from Heaven, morning star, son of the dawn! You have been cast down to earth, you who once laid low the nations! You said in your heart, 'I will ascend to heavens; I will raise my throne above the stars of God;

I will sit enthroned in the mount of assembly, on the utmost heights of the sacred mountains. I will ascend above the tops of clouds; I will make myself like the most high" (Isaiah 14:12-17 NIV). God knew what Satan was thinking even before God asked him what he was up to. The devil did not reply that his eyes were on Job, but God did. Lucifer thought to be like God. That is why God rejected him and cast him down.

Lucifer, Satan, the devil, has tried to prevent God's plan of salvation ever since the creation. He used kings to try to destroy the savior when Herod took the life of all the newborns in Bethlehem shortly after the birth of Christ, but he failed. We can understand that clearly in the book of Revelation. "A great and wondrous sign appeared in heaven: a woman clothed with the sun, with the moon under her feet and a crown of twelve stars on her head. She was pregnant and cried out in pain as she was about to give birth. Then another sign appeared in heaven: an enormous red dragon with seven heads and ten horns and seven crowns on his heads. His tail swept a third of the stars out of the sky and flung them to the earth. The dragon stood in front of the woman who was about to give birth, so that he might devour her child the moment it was born. She gave birth to a son, a male child, who will rule all nations with an iron scepter. And her child was snatched up to God and to his throne. The woman fled into the desert to a place prepared for her by God, where she might be taken care of for 1,260 days" (Revelation 12:1-6 NIV).

It is clear the child born was Jesus Christ and the woman symbolized the church. If we want to grasp that issue accurately, we can explore some of the Bible texts. "Wives, submit to your husbands as to the Lord. For the husband is the head of the wife as Christ is the head of the church..." (Ephesians 5:22-23 NIV). This verse shows there are comparable attributes or similarities between the woman and the church. Satan did not stop his attacks after the birth of Christ, but he continued to tempt Jesus and to tempt believers after Jesus completed the work of his father and ascended to heaven. Satan continues to attack Christians even today.

I might suggest that he is behind Job's story. But God is teaching us not to be upright in our own eyes when God blesses us with many things. Some think the only reason God fills their storehouse is because they did their homework, forgetting the favor of God upon them. A righteous person, rather, humbles himself, and if he repents, he will be saved. The story of Job reveals a possibility of sin even in a so-called perfect and upright man.

33

At the end of the story, Job repents and humbles himself. The Lord talks to Job out of the storm: "Brace yourself like a man; I will question you, and you shall answer me. Would you discredit my justice? Would you condemn me and justify yourself? Do you have an arm like God's, and can your voice thunder like his? Then adorn yourself with glory and splendor, and clothe yourself in honor and majesty. Unleash the fury of your wrath...look at all who are proud and humble them..." (Job 4:6-12 NIV).

Job mentioned the good deeds he had done and his pride in them when his friends came to sympathize and comfort him. However, God proved Satan wrong. Job did not fear God because he blessed him so much. But Job feared God because he trusted him.

Job's story also increases our knowledge of a passage in the letter of Paul to Titus: "He saved us, not because of righteous things we had done, but because of his mercy. He saved us through washing of rebirth and renewal by the Holy Spirit" (Titus 3:5 NIV). It is very important for Christians to know that good deeds are not good enough in the sight of God. God saves us not because of anything we do but only because mercy compels him to save us. If we received salvation through works we would be prideful and full of boasting. "Listen, my dear Christian brothers, God has chosen those who are poor in the things of this world to be rich in faith. The holy nation of heaven is theirs. That is what God promised to those who love him" (James 2:5 NLV).

Ironically, we learn from God's word that all people have been called but few are chosen. God chooses the poor to be heirs of heaven and makes them rich in faith. Heaven is not just for the poor alone, but also for all who love him. However, God wants to warn about the sin of favoritism and discrimination among Christians, turning them into judges of an evil thought. Being poor or weak does not represent the lack of faith, but the opposite is true. As a believer, being poor in terms of earthly, material possessions basically does impact your dependency on God and true believers are those who rely totally on God for daily provisions.

James asserted that Christians at that time in their churches trusted the rich with comfort but insulted and despised the poor. He warned them, "Is it is not the rich who are exploiting you? ...Are they not the ones who are slandering the noble name of him to whom you belong? If you really keep the royal law found in Scripture, 'Love your neighbor as yourself,' you are doing right. But if you show favoritism, you sin and are convicted by the law as lawbreakers. For whoever keeps the whole law and yet stumbles at just one point is guilty of breaking all of it. For he who said, 'Do not commit adultery,' also said, 'Do not commit murder.' If you do not commit adultery but do commit murder, you have become a lawbreaker. Speak and act as those who are going to be judged by the law that gives freedom, because judgment without mercy will be shown to anyone who has not been merciful. Mercy triumphs over judgment" (James 2:8-13 NIV). If you had a doubt about blasphemy and insults toward God and our Savior by those fortunate in terms of worldly resources, just turn on the TV in your living room.

"One hand full of rest is better than two hands full of work and trying to catch the wind" (Ecclesiastes 4:6 NLV). That man whose primary goal is to make money and pursues riches or wealth will, at the end, realize that his efforts drain his energy for the wrong purpose. God is the only source of wealth and riches. Faith and pursuit of God are true wealth.

Not all who believe in God will gain wealth, but they will not lack anything because God is a trustworthy provider. All things are possible to those who believe. Pursuing wealth will only cause us to **35** become exhausted. Busyness in order to store goods and money for the sake of comfort is a vain game. Wealth makes itself wings and flies away. "He who laughs at the poor brings shame to his Maker. He who is glad at trouble will be punished" (Proverbs 17:5 NLV).

When I was in recovery at the rescue mission, sometimes we came out of the building in order to shake off stress. We brought chairs out on the deck. As a matter of fact, the deck was facing the street, so people in the cars that passed could see us. Some drivers were probably just enjoying themselves. I do not intend to accuse everyone that passed the rescue mission of degradation. But there is a possibility that some of the people might have meant to be laughing at us. The Bible warns about laughing at the poor. People at the treatment center were not unfortunate, but they could be a laughing stock to those who did not understand their mission.

Many individuals are spending time and money to save lives by sponsoring these types of programs. I deeply thank God and hope he rewards them for their mercy and generosity. Jesus said in the book of Matthew, "Then the righteous will answer him, "Lord, when did we see you hungry and feed you, or thirsty and give you something to drink? When did we see you as a stranger and invite you in, or needing clothes and clothe you? When did we see you sick or in prison and go to visit you? The king will reply, 'I tell you the truth, whatever you did for one of the least of these brothers of mine, you did for me'" (Matthew 25:37-40 NIV). God will honor those who help the poor. We will not be judged by our faith but rather by our works, whether good or bad.

It is true that works do not save us. "For it is by grace you have been saved, through faith—and this not from yourselves, it is the gift of God—not by works, so that no one can boast" (Ephesians 2:8-9 NIV). God saved us; while we were sinners, Christ died for us. Christ's work of redemption and salvation was a gift from God. We do not have any credit whatsoever that made that happen. It happened only through grace and the mercy of God. But James says, "What good is it, my brothers, if a man claims to have faith but has no deeds? Can such faith save him?" (James 2:14 NIV).

Most Christians misunderstand the difference between redemption and salvation. I have been praying, trying to explain this issue because it is complex. I find it very complicated and ask you to pray for me about this issue and for the entire book. The Bible says there are paths that seem straight to man, but the end is death. Paul said there are different kinds of gifts, but the same spirit. There are different kinds of services, but the same Lord. There are different kinds of work, but the same God. Jesus said different talents will be determined by whether we have been faithful in his service.

Paul mentioned that no one can lay any foundation other than the one God has already lain, which is Jesus Christ. Jesus Christ did not limit himself to a single gift or talent, but rather he used all his talents and gifts. Therefore, if we want to be like Christ and have the spirit of Christ, we should not despise others saying service is not necessary for our salvation. Those who confess that salvation is not through work also should work or give to the needy, but not reluctantly as under compulsion, for God loves a cheerful giver.

Remember this: "God is able to make all grace abound to you, so that in all things at all times, having all that you need, you will abound in every good work. As it is written: 'He has scattered abroad his gifts to the poor; his righteousness endures forever'" (2 Corinthians 9:8-9).

"You foolish man, do you want evidence that faith without deeds are useless? ...As the body without the spirit is dead, so is faith **37** without deeds is dead" (James 2:20, 26 NIV).

Knowing that our salvation did not come through work should not stop the work of charity. We cannot work our way to heaven and we never will, but salvation by faith is not an obstacle to the work of charities. We should continue to help those in need according to our capacities, knowing that God promised when we do that we will not lack anything. "Tell those who are rich in this world not to be proud and not trust in their money. Money cannot be trusted. They should put their trust in God. He gives us all we need for our happiness. Tell them to do good and be rich in good works. They should give much to those in need and be ready to share. Then they will be gathering together riches for themselves. These good things are what they will build on for the future. Then they will have the only true life" (1 Timothy 6:17-19 NLV).

We should not feel intimidated or threatened by those who happen to be rich or wealthy, because the words of God give wealth and riches. The Bible states very clearly that stored riches can hurt a person and those who store riches for selfish purposes will even be prevented from sleeping. "He (Jesus) told them this parable: 'The ground of a certain rich man produced a good crop. He thought to himself, "What shall I do? I have no place to store my crops." Then he said. "This is what I'll do. I will tear down my barns and build bigger ones, and there I will store all my grain and my goods. And I'll say to myself, 'You have plenty of good things laid up for many years. Take life easy; eat, drink and be merry." But God said to him, "You fool! This very night your life will be demanded from you. Then who will get what you have prepared for yourself?" This is how it will be with anyone who stores up things for himself but is not rich toward God" (Luke 12:16-21 NIV). It is very clear from this verse that God is not pleased when we store riches for selfish reasons or purposes. We will bring judgment against ourselves. Also, we should share our wealth with others. God will keep his agreement and bless our children and our children's children for many generations.

Remember this: When God blesses you, do not intimidate others with it because this is wrong in God's sight. Some people do dumb things simply because they believe that wealth is a power. Do not be deceived by that. In the judgment of God, wealth will not save those who hold it. God is the judge of all; the weak and the strong. In our society today some of those who hold wealth think it is the real power; therefore, they make it hard for others to have the same opportunity.

The word "interest" is so popular in American society. But we believers have to be careful when people use that word. Ask yourself, whose interest are they referring to? If it is not the interest that would further God's work then it is not a right interest at all. The apostle Paul encourages us that everything we do, let us do it for the glory of God. In our culture today, people are more interested in those who have things. If they happen to be blessed with success, they only associate with those who are successful. They don't want to be close to anyone weak, sick, or homeless.

Here's how it works. If I had a professional job, I would not want to be anywhere near those who labor or work with their hands. I would not even encounter them unless I had an interest in something they could do for me. I would help those who were able to return the favor, in case you had some ability I might need in the future. I would draw myself to you for a healthy relationship knowing if I ever faced problems you would be able to help me. However, if you were weak or improvised I would not have anything to do with you.

If we call ourselves believers and we deal with people in that way we act like a sinner. "If you love those who love you, what reward will you get? Are not even the tax collectors doing that? And if you greet only your brothers, what are you doing more than others? Do not even pagans do that? Be perfect, therefore, as your heavenly Father is perfect" (Matthew 5:46-48 NIV). "He who makes it hard for the poor by getting more for himself, or who gives to the rich, will become poor himself" (Proverbs 22:16 NLV). The rich and the poor meet together. The Lord is the maker of them all" (Proverbs 22:2 NLV). "We came into this world with nothing. For sure, when we die, we will take nothing with us" (1 Timothy 6:7 NLV).

4

Sickness

In this modern time, we have witnessed drastic medical advances. There have been enormous changes in treatment of disease and illness. Medical technology has improved many aspects of human life. Certain ailments that in the past medicine could not heal now seem to be treatable because of technological advances. The United States spends a large amount of money in medical research to improve and save lives. However, the medical community still falls short and cannot cure all diseases. From the spiritual standpoint, according to the scriptures, some are the result of sin and some are not. What does the Bible say concerning healing?

"The rest of the oil in his palm the priest shall put on the head of the one to be cleansed and make atonement for him before the lord" (Leviticus 14:18 NIV). "Then he shall come out to the altar that is before the LORD and make atonement for it. He shall take some of the bull's blood and some of the goat's blood and put it on all the horns of the altar. He shall sprinkle some of the blood on it with his finger seven times to cleanse it and to consecrate it from the uncleanness of the Israelites" (Leviticus 46:18-19 NIV). If we accurately look at this verse, we realize the Priest cured the ailments the same way he cleansed the sin. The priest treated those who were ill similarly to those who committed sin.

God treated illness as sin, and those who were ill at that time are considered unclean. If diseases were treated as sin at that time they should still be treated the same way. I do not mean to judge or consider the ill person as a sinner. I am pointing out that God is the same God of yesterday, today, and tomorrow. If he was the source of healing in the past, he is still the source of healing today and tomorrow. I am not saying that all diseases are from sin, because I do not know. But God knows. Let me relate my story.

When I was home in Sudan, I had severed anxiety sometimes.

Although I was a believer in Christ, I could not cope or sleep. Suddenly, I came across a book that addressed anxiety. That helped me to deal with anxiety. Also, through reading that book, I came to discover that honeybees help with sleep. Therefore, every night before I went to bed, I would take two spoons full of honey. That, along with some exercise, helped me sleep well. Then when I left Sudan, I traveled through Ethiopia and Kenya where I started smoking and drinking. Finally, I ended up in the United States.

Two years prior to my arrival in the United States in 1997, I was diagnosed with mental illness (schizophrenia). Therefore, the doctor put me on medication which I took for almost twelve years. My experience with schizophrenia devastated me so much that I struggled with it every day. It sabotaged my work, my school, and robbed me financially, physically, emotionally, financially, morally, and socially.

Today I am free because I turned my life to God, in addition to support from my family and friends. Everyone can be free today if he or she will turn his or her life to God. He is the only source of healing. I believe that my mental illness was the work of the devil. The Bible relates to us in the Epistle of Mark the story of a man possessed by demons.

> They went across the lake to the region of the Gerasenes. When Jesus got out of the boat, a man with an evil spirit came from the tombs to meet him. This man lived in the tombs and no man could bind him any more, not even with a chain. For he had often been chained hand and foot, but he tore the chains apart and broke the irons on his feet. No one was strong enough to subdue him. Night and day among the tombs and in the hills he would cry out and cut himself with stones.

When he saw Jesus from a distance, he ran and fell on his knees in front of him. He shouted at the top of his voice, "What do you want with me, Jesus, Son of the Most High God? Swear to God that you won't torture me!"

For Jesus had said to him, "Come out of this man, you evil spirit!" Then Jesus asked him, "What is your name?"

"My name is Legion," he replied, "for we are many." And he begged Jesus again not to send them out of the area. A large herd of pigs was feeding on the nearby hillside. The demons begged Jesus, "Send us among the pigs; allow us to go into them."

He gave them permission, and the evil spirit came out and went into the pigs. The head, about two thousand in number, rushed down the steep bank into the lake and were drowned. Those tending the pigs ran off and reported this in the town and countryside, and the people went out to see what had happened.

When they came to Jesus, they saw the man who had been possessed by the legion of demons, sitting there, dressed and in his right mind; and they were afraid. Those who had seen it told the people what had happened to the demon-possessed man—and told about the pigs as well. Then the people began to plead with Jesus to leave their region.

As Jesus was getting into the boat, the man who had been demon-possessed begged to go with him. Jesus did not let him, but said, "Go home to your family and tell them how much the Lord has done for you, and how he has had mercy on you."

So the man went away and began to tell in the Decapolis how much Jesus had done for him. And all the people were amazed" (Mark 5:1-20 NIV).

If we accurately compared the behavior characteristics of the man who was demon-possessed in the Bible with a mentally-ill man, we see compatibility between them. The Bible mentions first that the man was living in tombs, could not be contained with chains, was very violent, and cut himself with stones. These kinds of behaviors are similar to those suffering from mental illness.

While I was in psychiatric wards at mental hospitals, I met many people who were there with me. I always formed a bond with them, trying to find out what brought them there. They all shared with me terrible stories about how they had almost committed suicide. One woman shared with me how she cut herself with knives, which caused her family to place her in treatment. Some of them told how they had been miraculously helped while trying to take their own lives.

I also met many who were homeless and on the streets due to mental illness. Most people suffering from mental illness, including myself, are loners. They love to isolate themselves from society, and that was exactly the condition of the demon-possessed man in the Bible. The scriptures mentioned that he was suicidal and negative. Many mentally ill people are easier drawn to break the law, which is the system of violence. If Jesus was able to bring a person like that to his senses and sanity, it is clear that prescription drugs cannot cure mental illness; only God is able to heal that condition.

During the years I was on medication, I tried many techniques and strategies that I thought would help me cure the disease, but all my efforts failed. One of my strategies was to enroll in college. I thought I needed knowledge to cure me because after I was affected by mental illness, I lost faith in God. I had what is known today by psychologists as poor self-image; low self-esteem or self-worth.

Many academies give false strategies about how to increase or improve our self-image. I am not trying to judge them. Many don't believe in God. I believe some academies may be faithful in their mission of improving lives, but man is a sinner and falls short of the Glory of God (Romans 3:23). "For since the creation of the world God's invisible qualities—his eternal power and divine nature—have been clearly seen, being understood from what he has been made, so that men are without excuse. For although they know God, they neither glorified him as God nor gave thanks to him, but their thinking became futile and their foolish hearts were darkened. Although they claim to be wise, they became fools" (Romans 1:22 NIV).

46

I once came across a book authored by a group of doctors who had collected research to find ways to cure mental diseases. Those great physicians revealed an enormous success in many cases, and the secret of their success was combining their treatment with the Word of God. I am not a physician and have had no training in the medical field. My mission here is to lead you to the true healer, creator, and the only one who saves lives.

From my personal experience, sin is the most dangerous disease. In finding ways to help me cure my illness I have read over a hundred books on a variety of subjects—for example; psychology, philosophy, and religious literature—to improve myself or my self-image, but all those dozen of books did not seem to help. I believe man cannot establish his self-worth by reading psychology or philosophy or anything else man could endow. But God can. When I first met Christ, it did increase my self-worth drastically. Realizing that I was a son of God changed my life. "To all who received him, to those who believed in his name, he gave the right to become children of

God" (John 1:12 NIV). My realization of the fact that when I received him I became the child of God strengthened my faith.

There is no disease God cannot heal. Some physical problems may be aided by a physician's help, but there are diseases physicians can not treat; for example, aids and mental illnesses. My standpoint is that they should be honest and refer people suffering from incurable diseases to priests or the church. "If anyone among you is sick? He should send for the church leaders and they should pray for him. They should pour oil on him in the name of the Lord. The prayer given in faith will heal the sick man, and the Lord will raise him up. If he has sinned, he will be forgiven. Tell your sins to each other. And pray for each other so you may be healed. The prayer from the heart of a man right with God has much power" (James 5:14-16 NLV).

In conclusion, I would suggest to you that if you have a mental illness, first find a church and ask them to lift prayers up on your behalf. Some Christian centers, like the rescue mission, have a variety of programs to help people recover from alcohol. Second, ask God to heal you. And if you have faith he will help you recover along the way. Paul advised Timothy to take a little wine for his stomach illness, but if you stop drinking you will be able to think clearly, because alcohol defiles the flesh.

5

Gossip

In our society today, many people find it hard to keep quiet. Gossip it is very popular. The Bible warns about it in Leviticus 19:16 (NIV): "Do not go around saying things that hurt your people. Do not do things against the life of your neighbor. I am the Lord." In our culture, people say things that destroy lives. They inflict wounds, either in the open or in secret. Gossip includes hurting people openly or indirectly. This is very common today, known as white lies or having fun.

This kind of talk is very serious sin in the sight of God. It is even adopted by religious leaders. A lie or a twisted meaning of a word or words could be very deceiving to your family, society, or church. Jesus talked about violence in the book of Matthew: "You have heard that it was said to the people long ago, 'Do not murder, and anyone who murders will be subject to judgment.' But I tell you that anyone who is angry with his brother will be subject to judgment. Again, anyone who says to his brother, 'Raca,' is answerable to the Sanhedrin. But anyone who says, 'You fool!' will be in danger of the fire of Hell. Therefore, if you are offering your gift at the altar and there remember that, your brother has something against you; leave your gift there in front of the altar. First go and be reconciled to your brother; then come and offer your gift. Settle matters quickly with your adversary who is taking you to court. Do it while you are still with him on the way, or he may hand you over to the judge, and the judge may hand you over to the officer, and you may be thrown into prison. I tell you the truth, you will not get out until you have paid the last penny" (Matthew 5:21-26 NIV).

Today, especially in our community, people are not respecting each other's feelings. Society is so corrupt, even kids do not respect the elders. But what I am explaining is what Christ taught about how family, community, church, even the nation should treat itself.

In old times the Bible talked about the murder. If a man killed someone he deserved to be dragged to the courts or subjected to judgment. Christ stressed that if a man was angry with his brother, it was exactly as if he murdered someone. However, if he called someone a fool, questioning that person's humanity or dignity as a child of God, he deserved to be thrown into the fire of hell.

I once came across a story related to me by an Egyptian Christian writer about children in an orphanage. It happened that some of their sponsors were invited to a celebration or party. A girl's teacher came to her room and asked her to go to the party and entertain her sponsor because she was very talented. She refused and rejected the idea. The teacher was furious and started attacking her and telling her she was worthless. That same night the girl hanged herself.

Words are sharp like a knife. I mean, hurtful words or insults may be stripping someone out of his or her dignity, rights, and worth. We are all children of God, whether males and females. God created us in his image no matter what our social condition. We are all valuable to our heavenly father. The bible warns us against talking about others in secret, because words tear the body apart. What is called gossip is a serious sin to our Heavenly father. "The words of a gossip are like choice morsels; they go down to a man's inmost parts" (Proverbs 18:8 NIV). "...A gossip separates close friends" (Proverbs 16:28 NIV). "A gossip betrays a confidence; so avoid a man who talks too much" (Proverbs 20:19 NIV). When you tell stories about others you make secrets known and by that you spread trouble, hurt people, and separate friends.

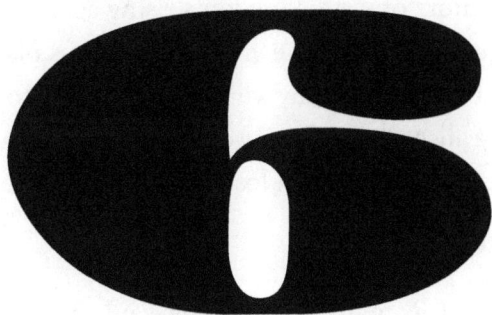

6

The Last Days

"As Jesus was sitting on the Mount of Olives, the disciples came to him privately. 'Tell us,' they said, 'when will this happen, and what will be the sign of your coming and of the end of age?" (Matthew 24:3 NIV).

Jesus told his disciples that in the last days many will come and deceive others by telling them they are the Christ. Also, there will be wars and rumors of wars, kingdoms rising against other kingdoms, and earthquakes shaking the ground in various places. But this will be only the beginning. Many will be handed over to persecution and be hated by all nations. Because of this condition, Jesus said love will grow cold and many will lose faith. But whoever will stand firm will be saved.

54

In the book of Romans, the Apostle Paul mentioned how people will be godless and suppress truth with their wickedness. Even though they know his mighty power, they will not glorify him as God. He says, "Therefore God gave them over in the sinful desires of their hearts to sexual impurity for the degrading of their bodies with one another... Because of this, God gave them over to shameful lusts. Even their women exchanged natural sexual relations for unnatural ones [what is known today as lesbianism]. In the same way the men also abandoned natural relations with women and were inflamed with lust for one another [known today as gays]. Men committed indecent acts with other men, and received in themselves the due penalty for their perversion. Furthermore, since they did not think it worthwhile to retain the knowledge of God, he gave them over to a depraved mind, to do what ought not be done. They have become filled with every kind of wickedness, evil greed and depravity. They are full of envy, murder, strife, deceit and malice. They are gossips, slanderers, God-haters, insolent, arrogant and boastful; they invent ways of doing evil; they disobey their parents; they are senseless, faithless, heartless, and ruthless. Although they know God's righteous decree that those who do such things deserve death, they not only continue to do these very things but also approve of those who practice them" (Romans 1:24-32 NIV).

The sin of gays or lesbians is no different from any other sin recorded in the Bible. Many people express a lot of hatred against gays and lesbians. But you cannot change anyone by shouting or hating him or her. A lot of political leaders and others are always demonstrating against gays and lesbians. The act of same sex marriage is an addiction like any other addiction, such as alcohol or cigarettes. However, it can be cured through AA and other support groups. AA meetings have proved to be very successful in most cases. Sometimes addicts experience a relapse, but they can straighten themselves up **55** if they want to.

The gay and lesbian lifestyle is a sin. It is a serious sin. So-called animal confrontations during sex are sin. Anal sex is common in this country. Unnatural relationships produce a lot of diseases, such as aids. Christians should not participate in this kind of lifestyle. This type of lifestyle is a sin toward our heavenly father but there is a chance for anyone who wants to change his lifestyle. However, Christians should not judge anyone else. We will all stand in front of our creator to be judged according to what we have done, whether good or bad. Some Christians put themselves in place of God by judging others. This is not right. Jesus said he came for those who are sick and wicked to redeem them, not judge them. Therefore, we should be supportive to any brother or sister who struggles with this sin and not judge them. So-called oral sex is also popular in our society today and we tempted in this way. But is it real? I do not think so.

When God created Adam, "The LORD God said, 'It is not good for the man to be alone. I will make a helper suitable for him... But for Adam no suitable helper was found. So the LORD God caused the man to fall into a deep sleep; and while he was sleeping, he took one of the man's ribs and closed up the place with flesh. Then the LORD God made a woman from the rib he had taken out of the man, and he brought her to the man. The man said, 'This is now bone of my bones and flesh of my flesh; she shall be called "woman" for she was taken from out of man.' For this reason a man will leave his father and mother and be united to his wife... The man and his wife were both naked, and they felt no shame" (Genesis 3:18, 20-23 NIV). Because God made woman from man's rib and we know the rib is close to the heart, a couple always wants to be close to each other.

There is a lot of sexual immorality in our society and a lot of addiction among us. We all have our part in the struggle against addictions.

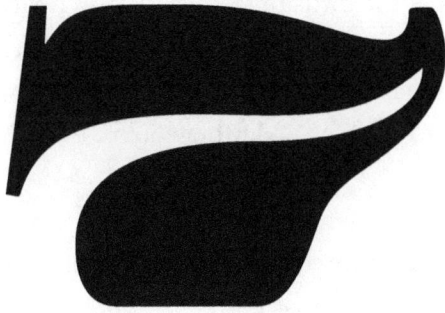

Anxiety and Depression

Anxiety and depression are very hard to encounter. These two enemies can tear you apart. When you are attacked by anxiety or depression it feels as if you are being pulled in two opposite directions. But the Bible gives us a weapon to conquer depression and anxiety. "Therefore I tell you, do not worry about your life, what you will eat or drink; or about your body, what you will wear. Is not life more important than food, and the body more important than clothes? Look at the birds of the air; they do not sow or reap or store away in barns, and yet your heavenly Father feeds them. Are you not much more valuable than they are? Who of you by worrying can add a single hour to his life?" (Matthew 6:25-27 NIV).

58 Depression and anxiety are tools the enemy uses simply to make us believe our lives are in our own hands. He uses this strategy to make us doubt the provision of God. We know God created us in his image and he sees us as valuable to him. God takes care of the birds and the animals; how in the world would he ignore our care? We tend to doubt his ability to care for us when facing a problem and we start worry and feel anxious about it.

Is it really worth worrying about? Worrying will not resolve the condition we are in. Instead, it will make us more afraid and irresponsible. If you feel attacked by anxiety always remember you are more valuable than the birds of the sky and believe God will resolve the issue no matter what it is.

"Where then is my hope? Who can see any hope for me? Will it go down to the gates of death? Will we descend together into the dust?" (Job 17:15-16 NIV). We know Job went through a horrible experience. The hurt that was inflicted on him caused him almost to lose hope and this is the form of depression. When we are depressed we lose hope in God and ourselves. We become unmanageable. But is the message of depression true? No, I do not think so. When we are depressed we see things not the way they are, but the way WE are. In addition, to convince ourselves that what we see is indeed reality, we deceive ourselves.

"From the ends of the earth I call to you, I call as my heart grows faint; lead me to the rock that is higher than I" (Psalms 61:2 NIV). In these verses, David addresses how he was depressed and anxious, but also stated in that he was climbing above his circumstances. This is the secret to defeating depression or other mental illnesses. We have climb above our current situation because when we climb higher anything underneath us looks small and that perspective allows us to prevail.

59

"I saw the tears of those oppressed—and they have no comforter... And I declared that the dead, who had already died, are happier than the living, who are still alive. But better than both is he who has not seen the evil that is done under the sun" (Ecclesiastes 4:1-3 NIV).

Outside influences cause most of the anxiety or depression we encounter. We might be depressed about what an employer or family member told us. But I have advice for you; those who are closest to us are the most hurtful, not because they hate us, but because they love us. So do not be aggressive when corrected by a manager or relative. The manager is always attracted to the person who does the job. The achievement of your boss depends on you, but if you make your existing power less than who you are you cannot benefit anyone.

"Therefore encourage one another and build each other up, just as in fact you are doing" (1 Thessalonians 5:11 NIV). God does not want us to be miserable, but rather he wants us to live an abundant life. He wants us to encourage and build each other. That means you don't need to live the life of isolation because when you isolate yourself from your friends and family you open the door for depression and loneliness. Therefore, being part of a family, a church, or a community plays a pivotal role in your growth and wellbeing.

Depression can turn into illness because those who confine themselves in their own narrow world away from their loved ones, family, and friends make their condition worse. Sometimes it makes it even harder to be cured. We are social beings; alienation makes us radicals or sociopaths. Those whose anxieties and depression turn into illness run from the realities of life. They tend to run away from family and friends. But that kind of behavior is so negative. No one can understand your illness more than your family. Family can give you support, insight, and an accountability you would never get anywhere else. Doctors can help you with medication but they cannot go beyond the family bond.

Anxiety could turn into serious depression if not handled properly. "Cast all your anxiety on him because he cares for you" (1 Peter 5:7 NIV). Realizing there is one bigger than your anxiety helps you cope. God wants us to know his greatness and acknowledge that he is the engineer behind creation. God understands how every organ in our body operates. He can renew the system. Failure to yell to God when we are affected with certain aliment contributes vastly to the failure of treatment. When we acknowledge that God created us with the purpose we can fight any illness that tries to slow or stop our mission here on earth. Therefore, we must learn how to deal with our fears and anxieties before it is too late.

Believe God in time of trouble and do not despise the help of the family and friends he has given you. They can be the source of strength. There are thousands of mentally-ill people on the streets and in government institutions in this country. The medical community strives daily for the recovery of these people. However, they find themselves inadequate to entirely cure the illness. They can only treat the symptoms. Personally, I am proud of their joint efforts to help these helpless people and I believe they are close to the root of the problem. Modern prescriptions pay an amazing dividend in treatment of mental cases.

Some of us worry about what others think about us, but Fay Walden, an English teacher once said, "Worry less about what other people think about you and more about what you think about them." Many people in our society are burdened about their self-image and how others perceive them. But this way of thinking, from my viewpoint, is absurd. You cannot accomplish anything in this life if you are obsessed with your self-image. Life involves taking risks even without **61** the approval of others.

Remember, even when you are in a social setting, you walk the path of life alone. You might not get where you want to go if you are always are concerned about your approval rating. The most superior and powerful people could be a source of strength for us. We can learn a lot from them if we stop competing with them.

Humility

Humility simply is willingness to recognize others for who they are. There is no partiality in humility. We humble ourselves in front of someone who is greater than ourselves at a given time. Also, for someone who is beneath us in some way, humility is caring and learning. We might encounter someone who is weaker than we are so we may be able to be helpful to him.

Humility is an education. It is tempting not to be resistant to someone who is higher than socially or economically because of jealousy. However, the humble person will swallow his pride in order to learn something. Prideful people are unable to humble themselves because they are obsessed with their own interests. They may think that if they humble themselves and lower their guard people will lose respect for them. The reverse is true.

Humble people are not threatened by others' status, education, or financial condition. They are content with what they have and they shape the history. "Samuel replied: 'Does the LORD delight in burnt offerings and sacrifices as much as in obeying the voice of the LORD? To obey is better than sacrifice, and to heed is better than the fat of rams" (1 Samuel 15:22 NIV).

There are four people in this world; (1) the man who knows and he knows that he knows—this man is hypocritical, (2) the man who knows and he doesn't know that he knows—this man is faithful, (3) the man who doesn't know and he doesn't know that he doesn't know—this man is foolish, and (4) the man who doesn't know and he knows that he doesn't know—this man is humble.

Humility is a learning process, if you are a leader and you do not put yourself in the shoes of your followers, your leadership will not be effective. True humility sees no difference between people. It regards the strong as important and the weak as the same.

I once worked for a telemarketing company. I worked so hard that I was awarded three certificates for perfect attendance. It happened that my boss found a job at one of the prominent Nissan dealerships in Salt Lake City. I decided to wish him good luck so I went to his office to thank him for his goodness toward me and tell him how thankful I was for his generosity in raising my salary three times within a year. As we talked, he told me he was happy for me for being humble.

Humble people are recognizable but they usually do not notice that people are observing them. That is why they are shocked when someone commends their humility. In Psalms we read, "He guides the humble in what is right and teaches them his way" (Psalms 25:9 **65** NIV). God loves the humble because in order to teach and refine us we must humble ourselves before him. The prideful person will not hearken to teaching.

There is a common phrase back home that goes, "The 'p' and 'i' will never learn." Those letters stood for "prideful" and "ignorant." Ignorance and pride are almost the same, because pride tends to ignore things and makes you passive at the same time. It would turn things down and leave it undone.

David said, "My heart is not proud O LORD, my eyes are not haughty; I do not concern myself with great matters or things too wonderful for me. But I have calmed and quieted myself, I am like a weaned child with its mother; like a weaned child I am content" (Psalms 131:1-2 NIV). In these verses David was referring to impossible goals. Some people set impossible goals that are out of reach and when they fail to achieve them they feel crushed and discouraged. We need to have logical and humble approaches toward our goals. For example, I am from Sudan and came to this country at the age of 23. It would be impossible for me to set a goal that one day I would be president of the United States because the constitution does not allow that. You cannot be president if you are not born in the United States. You can qualify to be a congressman if you meet the criteria and have great experience in politics and win the election, but not the president. That is impossible. An impossible goal can be part of pride. That is why when we share an impossible or out-of-reach goal, people do not tend to argue with us about it. They just laugh.

Our heavenly father hates haughty eyes. Ignorance is such a dangerous characteristic. Ignorant people miss a lot of things in life. They refuse to believe in anything. That is why they lack understanding. Wisdom and knowledge can be learned through humility. "Sitting down, Jesus called the Twelve and said, 'Anyone who wants to be first must be the very last, and the servant of all'" (Mark 9:35 NIV).

Humility is the spirit of servitude. "For all those who exalt themselves will be humbled, and those who humble themselves will be exalted" (Luke 14:11 NIV). When we humble ourselves, we are opening ourselves for the service of others and this act of service always is rewarded by God and others. A common phrase goes, "Do not praise your own self or boast about your intellect and abilities, but let others do it for you." Those who boast about themselves will be humbled. Life itself will humble us.

While we were in a refugee camp in Africa, one of my brothers-in-law got a letter from a distant relative who was living in Europe at the time. A phrase in the letter caught my attention. He mentioned that age was wise. After reading that short passage I found that it was absolutely true. We learn wisdom while going through life experiences. Some of us, as we are growing up, have no regard for anyone or anything. But the experiences of life—with its problems and obstacles—teach us how to humble ourselves.

Humility is not mediocrity. It is courage. Humble people are confident and courageous. Those who refuse to be taught by life become deviants and rebels. They have chosen to fight civilization with its existing regulations and laws that govern us. So humble yourself and you will be lifted or exalt yourself and you will be humbled. Some of us made enormous mistakes when young but we learned from experiences and correct our attitudes.

Those who refuse to take advantage of experiences are insane. The definition of insanity is to repeat the same actions and expect a different result. You never experience change until you learn to humble yourself. Humility is the first step toward recovery from addiction. That is why at recover meetings they start with admittance of their powerlessness against the addiction and the unmanageability of their lives. That is humility. When we humble ourselves, we are admitting that we are not perfect. We are acknowledging that we have not refrained from errors but we are willing to correct them.

Humility is a prerequisite for anything. It is required at work, marriage, family, church, and community. We learn the secret of inner happiness when we learn to direct our inner drives. We learn to focus our interest and attention toward something besides ourselves. Ethel Percy Andlus

9

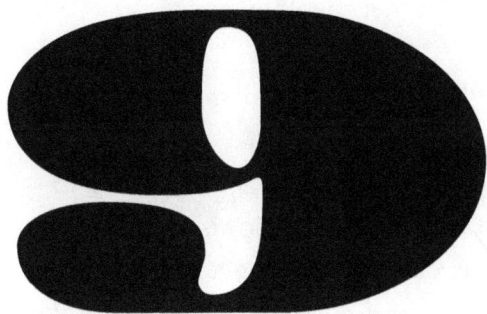

The Pursuit of Joy

The United States Bill of Rights declares: "We hold these truths to be self-evident, that all men are created equal, that they are endowed by their Creator with certain unalienable Rights that among these are Life, Liberty and the pursuit of Happiness." Individual rights and happiness are noble goals for any person or any nation to pursue. However, it would be great if the article read: "...all men...are endowed...with certain unalienable rights...and among them is the pursuit of joy" rather than happiness.

The word "happiness" comes from the word "happening." Our happiness depends on external causes; happenings. If something good happens I will be happy. So according to this view, happiness is not a permanent state. But joy is. If I am joyous it does not matter if things change or if something horrible happens to me. Happiness is external while joy is internal. David said in Psalms, "Shout for joy to the LORD, all the earth. Worship the LORD with gladness; come before him with joyful songs" (Psalms 100:1-2 NIV).

Joyful people are always optimistic about life. Their love reflects what is on the inside. Those who give others the joy around them receive happiness and joy in return. There is love and joy all around us but we cannot receive it unless we are willing to give it. Our heavenly father is delighted when we come to him with thankful and joyful hearts. When he created the first man, Adam, he said, "It is good." Therefore, after Adam fell into sin, God could have abandoned man forever. Instead, he provided again. He made a way for man to be at peace with him. The death of our Savior on the cross bridged the gap between God and us. Again, we can have a joyful relationship with him. Therefore, we can experience this wonderful joy and learn how to be glad at least most of the time.

You can cultivate joy by living a pure life. That will eliminate a lot of the depressing events and drama in your life. Many people choose not to experience joyful life by choosing to pursue selfish pleasures and evil purposes. God invented the family so we could live our lives to the fullest. Jesus reminded us in Matthew 6:22 (NIV), "The eye is the lamp of the body. If your eyes are good, your whole body will be full of light. But if your eyes are bad, your whole body will be full of darkness." The secret of cultivating joy will depend on how we look at things. The eye that wishes to have everything he sees on TV is an evil eye. The bad eye turns people to jealousy, hatred, and envy. In order to achieve that state of joy we must refine our eyes. Ask your heavenly father to give you a new eye that will fill your whole body with light.

We know that persecution could turn most of us to bitter and hateful. One psychologist once mentioned in his book that there are two things hard to deal with: hurt and hate. There is a possibility that a person who went through a divorce once will more than likely have a second divorce. The first divorce and the crisis that followed carried hurt and mistrust, and with it, hate and shame. Some learn to cope with this betrayal and learn to forgive and are able to have successful marriages in the future.

Family members sometimes feel persecuted by relatives because of under-achievement which frustrate family expectations. This happens often in our society today. Many are running away from family, relatives, and friends because they feel they are regarded as inferior or failures. Some disappear away from loved ones for years because they cannot overcome their inferiority. Therefore, they carry self-pity and seek revenge.

Jesus said in Matthew, "Rejoice and be glad, because great is your reward in heaven, for in the same way they persecuted the prophets who were before you" (Matthew 5:12 NIV). That is good news for you whether you are a believer or not. Do not let anything or anyone steal your joy. No one can ever ruin your life without your permission.

Some describe life as a battle or struggle. Others view it as a game or learning experience. No matter how you look at life, as one of my friends told me, find a way to enjoy it.

A teacher once asked his students about two people. One of them was chopping wood and the other sat reading. "Who is working harder," the teacher asked, "and how?" The student replied, "My father works in an office and chops wood for fun." No matter how things are going in your life, find time to be joyful.

72

The Bible declares that joy is one of the fruits of the spirit: "But the fruits of the spirit are love, joy, peace, patience, kindness, goodness, faithfulness, gentleness and self-control. Against such things there is no law" (Galatians 5:22-23 NIV). True joy comes from a deep spiritual life. The life of pleasure gives temporary flavor, a short buzz, but very quickly we find ourselves in a messy rut.

I once conversed with a Baptist minister who was delivered from addiction and drugs many years back. About the life of addiction, he said that whenever things had gone well for a while he would find himself asking, "What if I decide to use just once?" After he would accommodate himself with the first drug, the first would lead to next before he would collapse completely. In addition, he said, "Do you know, the strange thing about this dilemma is that I am always shocked when I find myself back in the same place which I left behind years ago: the same street, the same shelter I thought I would never see again."

"Rejoice in the lord always. I will say it again: Rejoice! Let your gentleness be evident to all. The lord is near. Do not be anxious about anything, but in everything, by prayer and petition, with thanksgiving, present your requests to God. And the peace of God, which transcends all understanding, will guard your hearts and your minds in Christ Jesus" (Philippians 4:4-7 NIV). The apostle Paul, in these verses, reveals that the secret of a happy and joyous life is to adopt the attitude of thanksgiving. There is a lot in your life you can be thankful for. Maybe it is a great relationship with your spouse, a decent family, or a great job. You can even thank God every morning for giving you another beautiful day. You can thank him for giving you the gift of life, just simply for being alive today. God has everything in store for those who believe in Him. It is really upsetting to God when his children go through life grudgingly, complaining about their problems. All we need is to look above and call for help. **73** Being anxious and burdened with our daily needs will not resolve our problems.

Jesus said, "Ask and it will be given to you; seek and you will find; knock and the door will be opened to you," (Matthew 7:7 NIV). Do we need more assurance than that promise? Of course not. Mother Teresa said that kindness can brighten our world. Kind words can be short and easy to speak, but their echoes are truly endless. Mother Teresa understood that we should not only be kind in deeds, but also in our words. She felt that the unwanted children in the streets of Calcutta, those rejected beings, didn't only need a warm bed to sleep in, but also a kind word to heal their wounds and hurt.

We all need to set that example in our world today. Kindness involves giving and caring. Kindness and caring could tame most of the hurts and suffering rampant in our world. Kindness could be assisting the needy on the sidewalk with a few dollars or giving a brief compliment to a co-worker or family member. Kindness also would include giving honest advice to the friend.

Many mistakes today could be prevented if we allowed those with more experience to advise us in some issues where our experience might be inadequate. Some people are offended when given advice because of pride. Individuals who "know it all" miss a lot of important lessons in life. Hannah Whitall Smith, speaker and author, was right when she said, "The true secret of giving advice is after you have honestly given it, to be perfectly indifferent whether it is taken or not and never persist in trying to set people right."

When I was in Salt Lake City, while heading to work, I saw a gentleman constantly sitting on the bench at the bus stop. He appeared to have no place to stay and he seemed to be on the street for a long period of time. One day when I came to the bus station as usual I decided to have a conversation with him. We exchanged a few words. I extended my hand into my pocket, grabbed a ten dollar bill, and gave it to him. He walked away happily and disappeared out of my sight. Some Americans are skeptical when they are approached by a complete stranger asking for change. I have met many of them. But it didn't seem to bother me to let go of a few dollars out of my pocket because I believe it would be very difficult to ask people on the street for a few dollars if you did not really need it. To me, sitting on a street corner asking for money would be the lowest state of poverty. Many people tell me if someone on the street asks them for money they would rather take the person to a restaurant themselves and pay for his meal instead of giving him money. They believe most of these people are con artists bumming money to spend on drugs or booze and coming back the next day asking for more. Limiting our generosity and service to charities will not be justified.

Our greed toward the needy on the sidewalk is condemned in the scriptures. "At one time we too were foolish, disobedient, deceived and enslaved by all kinds of passions and pleasures. We lived in malice and envy, being hated and hating one another. But when the kindness and love of God our Savior appeared, he saved us, not because of righteous things we had done, but because of his mercy. He saved us through the washing of rebirth and renewal by the Holy Spirit" (Titus 3:3-5 NIV).

It is a striking fact that our salvation is not our own. The mercy of God compelled him to do it. This holistic notion should be our model on behalf of those who still struggle to find identity in our cyber, high-tech world. Our world is getting more complex every day and moving at a rate faster than the speed of light. It is even impossible sometimes to maintain balance.

If you have plenty and are still miserable maybe you need to extend a helping hand to someone who is unable to repay you. That someone could be the next person on the street corner reaching out for a buck. In the Old Testament, our patriarch Abraham entertained angels without his knowledge and this act of kindness earned him redemption for his nephew, Lot, when the angels destroyed Sodom and Gomorrah.

Jesus also told the story of the kind and faithful who served him without knowing it by serving others. At the end of the day, Jesus compensated them by inviting them into his kingdom. He said, "Whatever you do to those little ones you have done to me."

I am not trying to say it is not sufficient to donate only to charities and you must start going to every corner in the city to find people who might need a dollar. Not at all. I believe we are saved through faith, through the mercy of God, not according to our goodness, generosity, or kindness. We cannot earn heaven. In addition, if those deeds are not a result of faith we do not have any sufficient amount of work that would guarantee life beyond the grave.

Once upon a time, I was watching a movie titled Wayne's World played by an actor named Mike Myers. In the movie I saw a sign that said, "No stairs to heaven." I was fascinated by that because the only way to heaven is through Jesus Christ. Jesus said in John 14:6 (NKJV), "I am the way, the truth, and the life. No one comes to the Father except through me."

This country, which I love the most, has almost completely combated hunger. Sometimes when I turn on the TV I am shocked about reports of a rare case about a few people going to bed hungry. When hearing this news, I usually find it hard to believe. The United States of America is the wealthiest nation on earth. And besides their wealth I realize that Americans are the most polite, sophisticated, and kindest people on earth. The generosity and kindness of fundamental Christians and those who sacrifice their assets for civil charities as well as private institutions have helped to address the hunger epidemic in America, this beloved country. Their efforts will not be ignored. When each of us spread acts of kindness we are not just pleasing others, but creating a better world for children, future generations, and ourselves.

A book I once read admonished, "Let us learn to give back a kind word or compliment and appreciate every moment in our lives." The author added that the Japanese appreciate art while Americans try to cultivate the art of appreciation.

10

Submission

Everyone needs to be valued. Everyone has the potential to give something back, from Diana, Princess of Wales, to the most unknown person, whether in the family group or in society at large. Each person is unique with different traits. Everyone may have a different method of dealing with others. But most importantly, we have a shared value.

There is nothing wrong with you being different from me. Our differences can be strength. As former US Secretary of State, Condoleezza Rice emphasized, everyone wants to be valued. Submission and respect for others are keys to the lasting realization of that value. No matter how you become closer to a person, without a stable boundary that relationship sooner or later will sour and become devastated.

Many conflicts begin when people cross these unseen boundaries. We need to respect others in order to be respected. Respect begins within us. Those who respect themselves tend to respect others. Realizing you are a valuable human being help you to respect others and their feelings.

Above all, or first, we must respect our heavenly father. After I began to grow in my knowledge of God I found myself nervous when someone profaned the name of God. Some people express their disrespect for God and disregard anything that involves spiritual matters. That always bothers me. Many of those people view God as a giant in the sky yearning to get us, and when we commit a sin, is anxious to strike us down and say, "Ha! I got you." Our heavenly father is not a critical judge roaring to find whom he may devour. We must slam the door of mistrust and doubt in order to be able to understand his true deity and his mercy toward us. From this moment forward, believe that God is your friend, not a judge working to throw us behind bars. Exodus 3:5 (NIV) reads: "Do not come any closer," God said. "Take off your sandals, for the place you are standing is Holy ground."

As we grow up, we gradually learn to respect others, whether it is their property or their privacy. Parents are so concerned about how their kids act in a public places, not because they don't want their kids to have fun but because they want their kids to know proper boundaries. They warn their kids about what to touch or what not to touch. Many parents yell at their kids when they are violating the privacy of others. This is to teach their children how to respect others. Basically, we learn respect at home. Those are the lessons parents instill in their children at the early age.

79

Tolerance is the greatest gift of the mind. It requires the same effort of the brain that it takes to balance oneself on a bicycle, said Helen Keller, the first deaf blind person to graduate from college. As children of God, our heavenly father makes sure we learn and develop caring matters that pertain to him. Whether we are presenting our gifts on the altar, sitting in church, or lifting prayers, God wants us to respect and honor him in everything.

Jesus, when giving the Sermon on the Mount, said, "You have heard that it was said to the people long ago, 'Do not break your oath, but keep the oaths you have made to the Lord.' But I tell you, Do not swear at all: either by heaven, for it is God's throne; or by the earth, for it is his footstool; or by Jerusalem, for it is the city of the Great King. And do not swear by your head, for you cannot make even one hair white or black. Simply let your 'Yes' be 'Yes,' and your 'No,' 'No'; anything beyond this comes from the evil one" (Matthew 5:33-37 NIV). All his life it was Jesus' mission to teach us and bring us closer to our heavenly father. He strongly challenged the Pharisees for their disregard of God. They appeared holy and righteous in the eyes of people while inside they harbored hypocrisy and deceit. Our savior rebuked them repeatedly for that double spirit.

In the old days, a life of disobedience and disrespect of God laws was a serious matter. It is still a horrible and despicable sin in our time. In the book of Exodus, God told Moses to make a basin for washing and instructed him about what Aaron and his children must do before entering the tent of the meeting. Whenever they entered the tent of meeting they had to wash their hands and feet and failing to follow those instructions would result in the penalty of instant death. "Whenever they enter the Tent of Meeting, they shall wash with water so that they will not die" (Exodus 30:20 NIV). Two of Aaron's sons, Nadab and Abihu, were consumed by fire when they offered unauthorized fire. Acting contrary to God's command, refusing to heed his instructions, was an act of disobedience.

How many people in our society today don't show remorse or fear when they revile the name of our Lord? How many Christians casually use the name of our Lord in vain and fail to respect the golden name of our savior and redeemer? Should we walk away from that person or could we challenge him? Some individuals disrespect the deity of our savior intentionally. What can we do about it?

Probably you don't want to be called a coward by Christ by denying him. But we must be careful how we respond. Peter drew a sword when the officer came to arrest Jesus in order to protect his master and prevent his arrest. But the Lord rebuked him. "'Put your sword back in its place,' Jesus said to him... 'Do you think I cannot call on my Father, and he will at once put at my disposal more than twelve legions of angels?'" (Matthew 26:52-53 NIV). It is so disturbing when so-called believers lead the band of war. If we indeed trust in God's protection, why should we worry about some kind of tyrant who hates our faith and our religion?

Believers should seek peace and stop beating the drum of war, not continue tapping it. Christians should seek peaceful methods to put out flaming fires and smoke that destroys our planet. We don't need tanks and weapons to defend our faith. Paul urged the people of Ephesus with these words: "Finally, be strong in the Lord and in his mighty power. Put on the full armor of God so that you can take your stand against the devil's schemes. For our struggle is not against flesh and blood, but against the rulers, against the authorities, against powers of this dark world and against the spiritual forces of evil in the heavenly realms. Therefore put on the full armor of God, so that when the day of evil comes, you may be able to stand your ground, and after you have done everything, to stand. Stand firm then, with the belt of truth buckled around your waist, with the breastplate of righteousness in place, and with your feet fitted with the readiness that comes from the gospel of peace. In addition to all this, take up the shield of faith, with which you can extinguish all the flaming arrows of the evil one. Take the helmet of salvation and the sword of the Spirit, which is the word of God. And pray in the Spirit on all occasions with all kinds of prayers and requests. With this in mind, be alert and always keep on praying for all the saints" (Ephesians 6:10-18 NIV).

Paul argued to take the word of God as the sword of the spirit, not an AK46 or 9ML. Why? Because our battle is not with the visible world or with flesh and blood. We are fighting an invisible enemy, Satan. Therefore, physical machinery or bombs will not destroy the evil in the world or sophisticated weaponry. Evil can only be rooted out through prayers and supplication. It is evil itself to try to protect religion or God. He is the all-powerful. The Bible says, blessed are the feet that bring the good news of peace. We should bring good news to our enemies, not hatred. Christians should not follow the secular society because we know that our home is not on this earth. Our heavenly home is made not with hands.

God is clear on this matter. The Old Testament book of Chronicles illustrates this through the story of a man called Uzzah. When he extended his hand to steady the Ark of the Covenant, he was struck dead. Uzzah's attitude angered God. From my point of view, we might ask why God should punish a man for protecting the Ark from damage. But God had made it clear no one was allowed to touch the Ark of the Covenant. God did not Uzzah's protection.

How many religions in the world are trying to force their faith on others? When Christ was here on earth, he did not preach religion. Religion is so dangerous when taken as rituals, culture, or beliefs. Christianity is more than religion. Christianity is a relationship. It is live communication between man and God.

God demands faith, obedience, and respect toward him. We do not need to continue using the name of God to achieve our pleasures and interests. Let us pray that the world would stop using the name of God for selfish purposes. We came in this world with nothing and we will take nothing with us to the grave.

As we saw in regard to disrespect and disobedience to earthly parents, God is our heavenly father and we also owe him respect and obedience. God spoke to Moses on Mount Sinai and told him anyone that cursed his father or mother must be put to death (Exodus 21:17). In modern time, insulting parents in their very faces has become common practice.

In our technological world the achievements of modern technology have made life easier. Electronic devices, such as cell phones, make it easier to communicate as far away as Africa to Afghanistan. We have found ourselves compelled to modernize the law of God. The laws of God are old, but Christians believe these laws are still relevant because they are right. Just because the invention of credit cards is modern doesn't make credit card theft right. Culture makes it feel right to go ahead with what is totally wrong. We should do things not because they feel or seem right but because they are right. The commandment says to honor your father and mother so that you may live long on earth. It is an old commandment, but it is modern in terms of context.

God will not reduce the penalty of disobedience to parents. A life of crime starts with little steps of disobedience. I am fascinated by the story of President Hinkley of the LDS church that just passed away a few years ago. President Hinkley, in his book, mentions after she heard him cursing, that his mother washed his mouth out with soap. That experience taught the Mormon prophet a lesson that guided 83 his spiritual life. Isabel Myers, a psychological theorist, correctly stated that we cannot safely assume that other people's minds work on the same principles as our own. All too often others do not reason as we reason, value what we value, or are interested in what interests us. We all are unique creatures with different principles and goals.

Children can be directed to a positive path. We cannot choose their careers or who they will marry, but we can help them make right choices, and the right time to do this is when they are young. The responsibility of training your child is not resting on the shoulders of your pastor or a teacher at school. You have the primary advantage for being a parent. Communication is very vital when it comes to a relationship with your child. Some parents distance themselves from their kids when they approach the teen years.

Some parents hide their own past lives from their children. They may fear being vulnerable if their child discovers their weaknesses. If you happen to be a single parent and you are a little bit low on the economic ladder, do not hide that from your child. It could strengthen your child's ability to make right choices. Cheering for them and maintaining communication are pivotal while children are young. At that point, they tend to believe anything parents or friends tell them. Talk to them frankly and in a loving manner about what could be the consequences of their choices. Unfortunately, some parents only react when kids have made an error.

Talk to them about the importance of staying in school and the disadvantages they will encounter if they do not. Talk to them about the danger of substance abuse. Many people who are casual drinkers or smokers who produce sober, healthy children. Don't stop talking to them about abuse. It won't make your message any less important because you are doing it. They will listen.

Some good Christians tend to talk to their kids when is too late. Speak to them while they are young. That will not guarantee they will obey and take your advice, but it will increase their chances of making right choices. "Children, obey your parents in the Lord, for this is right. 'Honor your father and mother'—which is a first commandment with a promise—'that it may go well with you and that you enjoy long life on the earth.' Fathers, do not exasperate your children; instead, bring them up in the training and instruction of the Lord" (Ephesians 6:1-4 NIV).

God requires submission to every authority instituted among men, whether to a government leader or our supervisor or manager because God placed authority for our own best and punishes those who do wrong. The bottom line is that we owe respect to anyone.

If you choose to disrespect yourself, others will do the same. We have to respect not only those who are in authority, but also those who are lower than ourselves. Anyone who disrespects kids, the kids also will treat them the same way. We need to learn to respect everyone—our teachers, our children, our wives, and our brothers and sisters.

Ephesians 5:21 (NIV): "Submit to one another out of reverence for Christ."

11

Attitudes

Let us say with Hilary Duff, "Mom always tells me to celebrate anyone's uniqueness." The dictionary defines attitude as a way of thinking, acting, or feeling. It is the manner or behavior of a person toward a situation or cause. Our attitude can determine and affect our life. If our attitudes are positive in any given situation it will increase our chances for success.

I am not suggesting you have to indulge and focus on your self-image in any given condition. When you obsess over your self-image your self-esteem can suffer. Rather, I am trying to enlighten you about the positive impact of your attitude. The German psychologist Karen Horney couldn't be more right when she said, "Concern should drive us to action not into depression."

Sooner or later we will find ourselves pessimistic. Optimists tend to avoid anything that could negatively affect their attitudes. Our attitudes are not determined by our altitudes. For those who claim to have a low self-esteem, their attitudes play a great role in that matter, because being disrespectful and hostile toward everything will not increase self-esteem. Instead, it will demean self-image.

People who tend to be dictatorial or authoritarian has been found to suffer from low self-esteem at the same time. Being permissive could also indicate low self-esteem. Therefore, it is our responsibility to protect our self-esteem from anything that will cause its destruction. Without a healthy view of self we will be unable to achieve or realize our proper significance. The word responsibility means to be able to respond and it our mission to be able to respond to anything which could undermine our self-esteem.

When Cain's offering was rejected, his self-esteem was hurt. God addressed this. "Cain was very angry, and his face was downcast. Then the Lord said to Cain, 'Why are you angry? Why is your face downcast? If you do what is right, will you not are accepted? But if you do not do what is right, sin is crouching at your door; it desires to have you, but you must master it" (Genesis 4:5-7 NIV).

How many people have not heard they were not good enough? Probably many of us are familiar with failed marriages. The final word is, "You are not good enough." Many young people have run away from families and loved ones because they were told they were not good enough. Many businesses have closed their doors because they were told their services were no longer needed because they were not good enough. No matter what the situation, what would be your attitude if you were told you were not good enough?

89

In this situation, Cain's self-esteem was tested by God. Unfortunately, he failed to maintain a positive attitude. God warned him about sin trying to master him. We today face the same dilemma. Whether relating with customers or loved ones, they have certain expectations and standards we are supposed to meet and when we fall short we face hostility.

It does not mean they are always right in their expectations, but the question is, what can we do about it? Some of our loved ones get hurt or experience loss due to our shortcomings. Their hostility might not be fair, but they feel that we have let them down. In the case of Cain, God told him, "If you do right will you not accepted?" Our attitude brings reward or punishment. We have to learn to maintain a positive attitude even when we are no longer respected. We need to forgive. God wants us to forgive even when others do not forgive us. By maintaining a positive attitude in any given situation, God can open a window. If God closes the door, he opens the window.

If you are being laid off because your company is downsizing do not walk out holding grudges but shake hands with your managers and thank them for letting you work at their company. By showing a positive attitude God will not keep you unemployed for long or maybe your employer will be able to call you back if the situation improves. Don't walk away cursing and angry. By doing the right things, God will cross you to the other shore. Paul exhorted the saints of Philippi, "Finally, brothers, whatever is true, whatever is noble, whatever is right, whatever is pure, whatever is lovely, whatever is admirable—if anything is excellent or praiseworthy—think about such things" (Philippians 4:8 NIV).

These verses sound like the inspirational messages we read in Dr. Norman Vincent Peal's books about the power of positive thinking.

This has been proven true by many scientific communities. Paul's exhortation is most needed in our violent world today. Storming our minds with positive messages boosts our attitude and increases our self-esteem. Narcotics and alcohol can destroy our self-esteem. In order to maintain a right mind and a healthy body we need to exercise and eat a balanced diet.

In the book of Colossians, Paul also encouraged the faithful brothers with these words: "Set your minds on things above..." (Colossians 3:2 NIV). The victorious life comes about by setting our minds on heavenly matters for the Christian, being more concerned about faith, love, forgiveness, eternal life, and things that pertain to our destiny than on negative circumstances that sometimes happen. Those who are burdened by pursuing earthly glory lose the meaning of life because this earth and its glory are fading. When we decide to accept the Christ as our lord and savior, our earthly life is hidden in Him. We come to understand that the flesh and its glory are temporary.

12

Embrace Your Dreams

"Hope shall live and the dreams shall never die." (President John F. Kennedy). The former president of Sudan, Jafar Mohamamed Nemeiri, was said to be the weakest student in all his subjects when he was at Hantub Secondary School in Sudan though he was known to be an excellent speaker and had a dream that one day he would become president of Sudan. When he revealed his dream to his peers he became a laughing stock to his friends. No one believed in him. But he believed in himself. He did not mind about being the weakest student in his class or having failing grades. Being from an improvised part of the country, his village had never before produced a college student. But Jafar immersed himself in student politics on campus and participated in many demonstrations and revolts around the campus. Surprisingly, in 1969, Jafar Niemerie became president of Sudan after a coup to overthrow elected Prime Minister Mr. Sadiq Almahadi.

We might not need to lead a coup to achieve our goals and dreams, but most importantly, we need to believe in ourselves first, and with the help of our savior, nothing is impossible. Maybe you held some dreams in the past, but now they seem to have dissipated. We might have failed to achieve some of our deepest dreams because we made wrong choices or because of illness or loss. It does not mean our world has ended. We read about many great men who have failed in different areas, but at the end prevailed and made history that shaped civilization and the world today. Some of these extraordinary men are President of United States Abraham Lincoln and Sir Thomas Edison. The reason these men were able to climb over their circumstances and succeed at the end was that they did not consider past experiences as failure but as learning experiences.

No one understood this more clearly than Kathleen Norris when she said, "Before you begin a thing remind yourself that difficulties and delays quite impossible to foresee are ahead. You can only see one thing clearly, and that is your goal. Form a mental vision of that and cling to it through thick and thin."

David said, "May he give you the desire of your heart and make all your plans succeed" (Psalms 20:4 NIV). Whatever our plans are, if we have faith, they will happen. God knows the heart of each one of us. If we persist enough to achieve, whatever we want, he will help us. Achieving our dearest goals requires commitment, persistence, and courage. Mr. Stephen R. Covey, in his book Seven Habits of Highly Effective People, mentions that all things are created twice. In order for an architect to build a house first he designed it on paper. We can consider that its first creation. When the building came into existence that was its second creation. All the plans were **93** written on paper before work actually began.

They say a journey of a thousand miles begins with a single step. Every goal or desire must start somewhere. God promised, "Those who plan what is good find love and faithfulness" (Proverbs 14:22 NIV). God helps those who participate in a good cause. He loves them and makes sure to guide them to right people who will open doors for them to achieve their goals. There are many good people around the world that desire to help those who want to contribute to humankind. Someone once said if you see a turtle up in a tree, you know he did not get there by himself. Those who shape history did not get there by themselves. Every word of advice, kindness, or help from a teacher along the way helped them climb those mountains. When plans are for what is good, God seals their destiny and guide them to faithful people who will assist them with the ladders to climb.

As we might guess, our minds are the battle ground and the enemy attacks our minds. Therefore, to withstand the evil arrows of the enemy, take the sword of the spirit, which is word of God. Whenever the enemy tries to convince you that you will not amount to anything, fight back with God's promises in the word. Expose him for who he is. He is a thief and the father of all lies. Claim what is yours. Our heavenly father has already pronounced us heirs with Christ. Dominion, power, life, death, everything you can think of is yours. God declared they are yours.

You have this promise in Job 42:2 (NIV): "I know that you can do all things; no plan of yours can be thwarted." To claim what is yours or to reclaim what has been robbed by the enemy is not going to be easy. It will involve a fight. No thief ever gave up without a fight, and no thief ever admitted to stealing even when they were caught in the act. Dr. John Garang said, "Therefore you need to prepare for battle and you need strong faith to retaliate. You cannot claim something you do not believe is yours. Do not indulge in self-pity and defeat. God promises no plan of yours would fail if you take it from the step of faith."

The Bible says, "The noble man makes noble plans, and by noble deeds he stands" (Isaiah 32:8 NIV). God call us to be kings and priests as a holy nation or chosen people. We are noble people called for noble deeds. We are a light to the world and soldiers of the cross, able to withstand the stronghold of evil. King Solomon encourages us with these words: "Make plans by seeking advice; if you wage war, obtain guidance" (Proverbs 20:18 NIV). To achieve your goals requires a road map and that involves plans. Most successful plans succeed through wise advisors. Snap judgments always lack momentum. Some goals can be achieved in a short amount of time but some may take a lifetime. That is why it is important to choose your goals carefully.

Do not plan unattainable goals because if you fail you will become discouraged. There is a thing we cannot plan. Some things are out of our reach; for example, who we will fall in love with and marry, whether our firstborn will be male or female. Be reasonable in your goals.

A few years ago I had a girl whom I loved back home in Sudan. I was very attracted to that woman. When I first came to this country, I said, "Yes, she is mine." Fortunately, I was in a position of power more than those still home who might have been interested in her. Because I was in United States, I was capable of funding whatever cost the marriage would require due to the vitality of the dollar against the Sudanese pound. You might be a little off about what I just mentioned, but in fact, marriage in Africa is different from the American system of marriage. In Africa, the groom must pay assets **95** in terms of herds of cattle to be considered as an official marriage. However, I fell short and failed to obtain my bride because I was diagnosed with mental illness and was unable to hold a job.

The reason I relate this story is not to gain your sympathy, but rather to prove to you that some things unplanned might happen. However, that is okay because God has something better for you. I believe deep inside that when God stops you it is because he has something better.

I repeat: If God stops you he has something better for you. If he stops your marriage, he has someone better for you. If you plead to God every night about that job and do not get it, do not stop pleading. He may not give you the same job, but he will grant an even far better job. Paul pled with God several times to remove the thorn in his body. Instead, God told him, "My power in weakness is sufficient." This means that some of our weaknesses could be the source of our strengths. Sickness could be blessing in disguise. Losing a job could be a blessing in disguise.

Someone might have dreamed for a long time about writing a book, but could not get the chance to write it until he got laid off. Someone might not have thought that one day he would make it to becoming a bestselling author until he was diagnosed with cancer. God is the master planner and organizer. We will never fully understand his thoughts or mind except what he reveals to us in his word and what his Holy Spirit reveals to us. Trust God with all your heart and do not lean on your own understanding and he will direct your path. Delight in him and he will give you the desires of your heart. His ears are not dull to hear, nor is his hand short to save. But our iniquities have separated us from him.

96 Please meditate on this beautiful word: "Blessed is the man who does not walk in the counsel of the wicked or stand is the way of the sinners or sit in the seat of mockers. But his delight is in the law of the LORD and on his law he meditates day and night. He is like a tree planted by streams of water, which yields its fruit in season and whose leaf does not wither. Whatever he does prospers" (Psalms 1:1-3 NIV).

My brother, meditation on the word comes with heavy price. Meditation on God's word will shut down any evil thought or negative message the enemy uses to bombard us with every day. He will take advantage of all available mediums, whether humans, radio, TV, or computer. He will do anything to catch our attention. "The beast was given a mouth to utter proud words and blasphemies and to exercise his authority for forty-two months. He opened his mouth to blaspheme God and to slander his name and his dwelling place and those who live in heaven" (Revelation 13:5-6 NIV).

To the beast, which worked with the power of Satan or Anti-Christ, will be given a mouth and authority to control the earth. I deeply believe that the only way the beast will be able to open his mouth is through those mediums I mentioned above. Through this message, we believers are warned about our attitudes toward the things we see and hear. I do not want to entirely demonize radio, TV and the Internet. But we must select them with care because they stay with us. Certain exciting programs filled me with joy when I was a child and I still remember those shows.

In our modern day, the TV is not advancing our moral values, and more shockingly, those who perform those programs are regarded with respect and honor. It is outrageous. This wars against our dignity as a child of God and also erodes our moral values.

God will let us achieve goals even beyond any we may want to achieve **97** if first we purpose to please our savior.

13

Race and Courage

Silent film actor Dorothy Bernard once said, "Courage is fear that has said its prayers." But when I came back at the dictionary to define courage, it listed fearlessness, or meeting a danger without fear, moral strength that makes a person face any danger, trouble or pain steadily without showing fear. I like that last definition most because being courageous doesn't mean being without fear when facing a situation but rather being guided by a moral strength that equips you to deal with that situation without showing the fear.

It was never easy for Yuuri Gagagareen being the first man in space, but that was courage. To be the first person in your family to graduate from college does not come without a price, but that is courage. It was never easy for Barack Obama to run for president of the United States while many believed blacks were not ready to lead America, but he ran and won. That was courage. Mary Robinson became the first female elected president of the Republic of Ireland. That was courageous. It takes a lot of faith in yourself to be able to do something many believe can't be done.

Many things seem impossible when we view them from our human understanding, but there nothing impossible for people who believe in God or have faith in him. Those who trust in God learn to have confidence that God will grant them anything according to his will. Jesus told his disciples that if they had the faith of a mustard seed they could command the mountain to move and it will obey them. There is nothing impossible for people of faith. It takes one pat on the back to keep you moving. Moses, after the Lord told him he would not be able to lead the children of Israel into the Promised Land, was told that Joshua would take his place. So Moses began to encourage him with these words: "Be strong and courageous. Do not be afraid or terrified because of them, for the LORD your God goes with you; he will never leave you nor forsake you" (Deuteronomy 31:6 NIV). God is a God of opportunities and strength. The children of Israel understood that it would not be an easy journey to the Promised Land, but even though they doubted him many times and murmured most of the time in the desert, our heavenly father walked with them through the entire journey. God never stopped encouraging them. He walked with them and fought their wars.

Sometimes when we sink to the bottom of our problems and circumstances we become pessimistic and forget that God also bears our burdens with us. Our heavenly father loves us so much he never forsakes us or leaves us alone. I am impressed by the courage of southern Sudanese leaders. Despite their higher education and achievements, they left their professions in North America and **101** Europe and engaged in gorilla fighting with the Sudanese regime. People like Dr. Gerange the Decess, founder of SPLA, Sudanese People's Liberation Army, and Dr. Riak Machar, Dr. Lam Akol and others are primary examples of courage. Their sacrifices have resulted in the birth of a new nation in southern Sudan.

The courage of one person brought reconciliation in America. Dr. Martin Luther King, through the civil rights movement, encouraged the integration of all classes and castes and changed the image of the United States around the world. In addition, the courage of President Obama improved the image of the United States all over the world. Instead of having a bad view of America as a wild beast that strikes wherever he pleases, the participation of different races in American government or leadership will strengthen the American Democracy and ensure the American leadership in the world.

In the 90's I read an article by an Arabian writer in an Arabic newspaper about his grief about their involvement in the destruction of Soviet Union. When looking back, many Arab elites think America is worse than the Soviet Union and that they were safer when the Soviet Union existed. However, through President Obama's courage and beliefs many nations have started changing their perceptions about America. There are many revolts throughout Middle East regions today because of the emerging New America. Many nations want to readjust their position toward America. Even the Chinese president-elect decided to visit Washington and meet with President Obama.

Our Savior, Jesus Christ, left his throne above to come down to earth and take human flesh so that he could redeem the flesh of humankind. That was courage. With pain and weakness, I once watched a documentary about Libyan resistance to Italian colonization in 1988. Omar Mocktar, a Libyan patriot, waged a courageous war which ended by Italians capturing him. He was executed, but his execution ended colonial rule in Tripoli. It brought freedom and independence in Libya. That was courage.

Courage is to keep going despite failure. You might have heard the story about a Jewish man known as Victor Frank who was placed by Nazis in a concentration camp in Germany where six million Jews perished. Miraculously, a few survived and Professor Victor Frank was one of them. When he wrote a book about his experiences in that horrible place, it became obvious that it is possible to survive even in the most horrible conditions if you choose your reaction wisely. As we know, the matter of racial conflict is a global phenomenon. There is not a single minority group in any country that would claim they are the only group to be victims of racial discrimination. In addition, we learn that there are minorities even within dominant majority groups. Therefore, I personally cannot confine the matter of race to a single box.

When I was growing up in Sudan, I was fortunate to study in the best schools in Northern Sudan. After we moved to the capital,

Khartoum, in 1987 I was enrolled in one of the junior high schools in a suburb of Khartoum where we were living. I saw that many people chose to react differently to the race matter in Sudan.

Sudan is the largest country in Africa, rich in many resources on the surface and under. First it was a colony of Turkey, followed by Britain. Anglo British-Egyptian authority divided Sudan into two different regions, one in the South and another in the North, so British authority established Khartoum as capital. They established a base or a camp of operation to strike any inside or outside opposition. In addition, they authorized the law of movement so in order to go to Southern Sudan you were required to present a visa. The British were trying to maintain the rule of the two nations **103** under one umbrella. They succeeded in ruling Sudan for decades and established the civil administrations and educational systems until the Mahadist movement broke out. However, the Mahadist movement headed by Mohamed Ahmed El Mahdi did not pose much of a threat until the Second World War broke out in Europe. Most of the countries through the Black continent and some of the Middle Eastern countries took advantage of that condition and resisted mightily. Colonial rulers throughout the globe decided to withdraw from their colonies because conditions back home were not okay. The British decided to make an agreement with resisting powers and granted independence to the Sudanese.

Now we come to the Southern rebellion. According to some Sudanese writers, the transition government led by Ishmael Alazhar did not include the south in the institution. When asked why, their answer was that southern Sudanese were lacking in the expertise and experience required in these institutions. This betrayal was interpreted by southern Sudanese as a new way to colonize the south and replace the old master with a new one. The first southern rebellion broke out in a small town known as Towreet in 1955 led by the group from the Equatorian region. This rebellion lasted for sixteen years and was ended by the Adiss Ababa agreement known as the Addis Ababa accord of 1972 hosted by Ethiopian president Mayla Salasi. Shortly after signing the agreement there was a revolt or mutiny in Akobo, a town in the Southern Sudan. Before it broke down, Mr. Honorable Abel Aliar who was acting as president of southern Sudan at the time, commissioned my father, who was a minster of the region administration, to accompany Mr. Peter Gatkoeth Gual to calm the situation. Fortunately, the mission was successful and stopped the rebellion.

The southern Sudanese marriage of pleasure and self-determination lasted until 1983 when John Garang defected and joined the faction in upper Nile led by a small officer, Mr. Samuel Gai tut. Doctor Garang seized the leadership of the SPLA movement, the Sudan People's Liberation Army, which brought recent and final agreement known as a Comprehensive Peace Agreement or CPA, which would finally lead to succession of the south and birth of a new nation on the Nile. The race matter in Sudan was fueled not only by differences in ethnicity or color but also religious differences played a pivotal role and widened the gap between the two foes.

The separation of Sudan is a sad dilemma to many Sudanese from both sides, including me. Some politicians from both sides of the isle tried hard to prevent the division of the country. Many southern and northern people have lived side to side for generations despite the ongoing war. For two decades Sudanese from both sides lived in harmony. Southern politicians such as the honorable Abel Aliar tried harder and harder to resolve the Sudanese conflict. He was one of the key players in the Addis Ababa agreement and in this recent agreement. Mr. Aliar remains a national icon in the Sudanese arena. Matthew 5:9 (NIV) says, "Blessed are the peacemakers for they will be called the sons of god." Those who remain peaceful in the face of persecution are courageous people. God is a just God and when we neglect justice we are even worse than the sinners. However, justice should not proceed from hateful intention. It should be channeled through means of love.

The apostle Paul mentioned in 1 Corinthians 13:4 (NIV), "Love is patient." What about anxiety and depression? Stress is a disconnection from the earth and forgetting of the breath. Stress is an ignorant state. It believes that everything is an emergency. Nothing is that important. Just lie down.

Natalie Goldberg, author and teacher says, "Some people assert that a little anxiety or worry is necessary because it compels us to get **105** something done. Worrying about upcoming exams could motivate you to study a little bit more, but stressing out often could severely negatively affect you; it could deviate into an illness, phobia or panic attack." There are many things that can trigger our anxiety; for example, going to an interview for a new job or going on a date, chariots of gods, UFOs, saucers/ancient aliens. Extraterrestrial.

I Corinthians 13 continue, "...Love is kind. It does not envy, it does not boast, it is not proud. It is not rude, it is not self-seeking, it is not easily angered, it keeps no record of wrongs. Love does not delight in evil but rejoices with the truth" (I Corinthians 13:4-6 NIV). Race will exist until the dawn, but it must be addressed wisely in the spirit of truth and must be combated in our churches or societies where we live. In the early church some of the Greek women complained about racial problems. The disciples managed to resolve the issue immediately. "In those days when the number of disciples was increasing, the Grecian Jews among them complained against the Hebraic Jews because their widows were being overlooked in the daily distribution of food. So the twelve gathered all the disciples together and said, 'It would not be right for us to neglect the ministry of the word of God in order to wait on tables. Brothers, choose seven men from among you who are known to be full of the Spirit and wisdom. We will turn this responsibility over to them and will give our attention to prayer and the ministry of the word" (Acts 6:1-4 NIV).

The race problem existed from the early age. Christians or believers should concentrate on prayer and the ministry of the weak in their societies. It takes men of courage to address the issue of race in a civil and proper manner. Dr. Martin Luther King, Jr.'s deep faith in God and love compelled him to lead a million-man march. His courage and love brought reconciliation to all American people. Some African Americans complain about the social integration that has been achieved by the civil rights movement asserting that it inflicts hurt upon Black America instead of improving it. The African American Professor Cornell West of Princeton spoke about this in his book Race Matters. He mentioned that in a book titled Anatomy of Black Conservatism the author asserted that race in America is not confined to those low on the economic ladder, but even black politicians are affected by racism. Their white peers look upon them with disdain and consider them as unqualified leaders. The only way they can make it to their positions is through Affirmative Action. The Powermatic National Plan for the Black race to combat poverty is a positive strategy to combat racial discrimination. I believe Dr. Claud Anderson has a modern broader view to resolve race anywhere or in any place.

Someone might ask me why I am writing about the problem of race. During my sixteen years of living in the United States I have faced many racial incidents at work and in other social settings. In Salt Lake City, when I arrived in this country in June 1995, I did not feel hatred toward anyone even though I am Sudan where many of southern Sudanese people deal with racial incidents every single day. I was fortunate to not experience those conditions. My coming to

106

America was for economic reasons more than persecution. I do not mean to claim that Sudanese immigration to the United States is totally because of economics or persecution. I do not want to be prideful to say I would even stand aside and look while many of my people are persecuted. I left home at age of twenty-one without experiencing racism because of my social and economic status. However, when I arrived in the United States I found myself rejected by all groups.

Being part of a community means to contribute something to the society in which you are living. The incident that hurt me most happened two weeks after my arrival to Salt Lake City. When I met someone, no matter from what group—Black or Caucasian—I would engage them in fruitful conversation with an excited, loving spirit. But at the end of the conversation they would turn around and bite me in the foot with the questions such as, "Did you ever see a leopard where you were living?" or "I want to visit Africa because I want to see some animals." I am always shocked, and more importantly, hurt and feel betrayed by a person who turns out to be a con artist who pretends to be interested in my conversation and I find myself answering questions. How could a person ask me such horrible questions and not even know me? He does not know anything about where I grew up or what kind of family I came from. He thinks because I am from Africa he has the right to make that kind of statement, even educated people and people you thought were important to you. When growing up in Sudan, I never knew racism and now I still see people who overlook others as sick or uncivil. God created man in his own image and that distinguishes him from animals. I perceived racism as a sign of weakness and inadequacy and is indirect violence and rights abuse.

When I was in high school, I came to have a Christian literature tract. One of the issues the author shed light upon was human rights abuse. The author told the story of a young girl who was very talented in singing. One day a sponsor was invited to an occasion made in their honor. Her teacher went to her room and asked her to come to the podium and entertain the guest. The little girl responded that she did not feel well so she was unable to grant the request. The teacher was not pleased with the response. She became furious and started attacking the girl and telling her she was not worthy and those people were housing and feeding her. The teacher continued yelling at the girl about how disgusting and worthless she was. The girl rushed out and committed suicide that night.

In the epistle of Matthew, Jesus said anyone who murders will be subject to judgment, but anyone who call someone else a fool will be in danger of the fire of Hell. Jesus considered degradation or disdain toward another human worse than taking someone's life. When you call someone a fool you not only hurt his flesh, you destroy his soul as well. How many kids turn out to be criminals and deviates because their families, teachers, or friends told them they were not good enough or that they were fools? Race turns hearts to hate and when you allow hate to take control that opens the door to self-pity and self-pity is a life-sentence.

The second reason that forces me to write about the matter of race is that I love America and all Americans despite their races and I do not want to stuff my anger and fears because there is no fear in love and perfect love draws away the fear. There is no fear in love. Love builds, it does not destroy. Hate destroys, but love builds. Being part of American society, I would not allow myself to be involved in a matter that would divide America. I would engage in issues that would increase solidarity among American people.

The third reason I am compelled to write about this issue is the negative spiral or downward mobility taking place in our communities. Most Sudanese consider the United States a Good Samaritan that gave them new hope after decades of war. The majority of Sudanese choose resettlement in America rather than European countries, Australia, or Canada because they believe deep inside that the United States is the land of opportunity and freedom. However, what happened to those opportunities? In disillusionment, some Sudanese men commit suicide and leave behind their children. Why are Sudanese, even females and teens, turning to drugs while those practices are not common in their homeland? I would not estimate the role of racism in their involvement in derivate acts, loss of hope, and absence of purpose.

In Salt Lake City, I was chatting at the Sudanese store when someone **109** related to me the story of a young Sudanese man who worked at the meat plant. He had stabbed himself several times with a knife because he was upset about repeatedly being treated unfairly. I heard about another incident that happened at meat plant in Lincoln, Nebraska. A young Sudanese man opened fire on several fellow-employees, killing one and injuring six. This negative picture now emerging in our community really hurts me deeply.

In 2007, it happened that I was working at one of the phone companies in Salt Lake City, Utah. Four brothers from Sudan along with three other brothers with one sister worked with me. In those days president Obama was campaigning for the highest office in America. While introducing themselves in a meeting, all those brothers said they would likely vote for Hillary Clinton. Many African American accused African nationals of being pro-white. I met some brothers here in Atlanta and whenever I tried to talk to them they would engage me on racial issues. Mostly, they accused us of being treated better in America than they are. That is absolutely not true, but we choose a different course to deal with the situation. Some Sudanese are successful in America, some for some it did not work. Some have decided to go back home and many plan to go back in the next couple of years. Their biggest complaint was that they were underpaid. That is not necessarily seen as a matter of race. But some decide to go home because they feel the race problem. I would support that action rather than what the Sudanese man in Lincoln, Nebraska did by shooting innocent people. That was a horrible crime. It was not an example of the right way to approach the racial problems in America.

My father was born in a small village in southern Sudan. As an adult, he moved to the city. But he refused to live a life of mediocrity. He took a job as a small officer. He indeed went through what every southern Sudanese went through at that time, but he refused to be bitter and hateful. Without a college education, my father became one of the most trusted civil servants. President Mohamad Neimeiri trusted him with hard issues in the country. In 1972, the people of Darfur region repeatedly opposed the government regarding tax policies. They refused to pay taxes to the government. That issue posed the threat to Khartoum. But there was one man the president trusted and knew very well to get things done, and that man was Moses Choul. President Jafar Nemier said, "I would send him," and surely, he got the job done. One of the stories I heard about my father was that when news reached President Jafar Nemieri about his death, he had tears in his eyes and said these words: "Indeed, we lost a great man."

Going back to racial matters, it is wrong to treat a person next to you with hostility because he refuses to live the life of hate. Those who address the issue of race in America are not necessarily focused on race. Rather, they want to enhance and improve American society. I would not deny the pain some of our ancestors had to go through during the time of slavery in this country, as well as modern slavery at my hometown in Sudan. Many southern Sudanese have experienced harsh treatment being taken into slavery by an Islamist militia. These modern day acts of slavery in the south angered many Christians in the west.

In one Sudanese documentary on slavery in the Sudan, I watched one a British activist rage while trying to free some of the helpless people from my country. President Bush signed the Sudanese Peace Act and assigned the Reverend John Danforth. This humble man whom I admire was able to accomplish something the Sudanese themselves had failed to achieve. That shows the wisdom and humility of a man whose heart is filled with the love of God. I believe Mr. Senator knew that there is nothing impossible for those who are in Christ. If God is with us, who will be against us? Through my exploration of hundreds of books on a variety of subjects by different American authors, I see that race cannot be combated by guns and violence. The civil right movement of 60's reduced racism and hostility in America, but it failed to produce quality of life in terms of financial economic reparation or equality of economic assets.

Some hostility we face is of our own making. For example, if a person chooses to neglect education he finds himself at a certain corner shooting at a cop or a respectful citizen. Racism has nothing to do with that. But racism is real in any society. For example, in Sudan race matters center around different tribes competing for land resources. Just because Sudan is tribal it did not differ from any other nations in the world. For example, in United States the president is elected by majority vote, and that majority includes all.

14

Love

When I look at the dictionary for the definition of love, it is defined as fond or tender feeling, warm liking, and affection. But when we look at the Bible, love refers to charity. Charity is strong relationship not related to sex. Charity is an unconditional love. When we look at this topic in the light of the Bible, we find the excellent way.

"If I speak in the tongues of men and of angels, but have not love, I am only a resounding gong or a clanging cymbal. If I have the gift of prophesy and can fathom all mysterious and all knowledge, and if I have a faith that can move mountains, but have not love, I am nothing. If I give all I possess to the poor and surrender my body to the flames, but have not love, I gain nothing. Love is patient, love is kind. It does not envy, it does not boast, it is not proud. It is not rude, it is not self-seeking, it is not easily angered, it keeps no record of wrongs. Love does not delight in evil but rejoices with the truth. It always protects, always trusts, always hopes, always perseveres. Love never fails. But where there are prophecies, they will cease; where there are tongues, they will be stilled; where there is knowledge, it will pass away. For we know in part and we prophesy in part, but when perfection comes, the imperfect disappears. When I was a child, I talked like a child, I thought like a child, I reasoned like a child. When I became a man, I put childish ways behind me. Now we see but a poor reflection as in a mirror; then we shall see face to face. Now I know in part; then I shall know fully, even as I am fully known. And now these three remain: faith, hope and love. But the greatest of these is love" (I Corinthians 13:1-13 NIV).

In fact, love came from the Greek word "agape" or unconditional love. Another name for love in the Bible is "fileo" or brotherly love. Love is an important organ that connects man's soul with his body because when we love we can change other things. There is a difference between pleasing someone and loving them. Someone who yearns for acceptance by society or a friend intends to please them. They can even be happy around them while trashing and profaning the dignity of others. That it is not love at all. I call this "love please."

Verse six says that love does not delight in evil, but rejoices with truth. Sometimes we are afraid to correct someone who is doing wrong even if we feel uncomfortable going through the experience. That is sin. The Bible says whoever knows how to do good and cannot do it, to him it is a sin. We see some of our family or friends indulging in gossip or slander or even profanity but we do not have enough courage to tell them it is a sin. It does not take a long lecture to correct someone. It can take only two or three words. And if that does not do the trick maybe it is time to break away from that person. Because love does not delight in evil, it is possible that our life would be full of joy and happiness every single day because Christ said I came so that they may have life and that more abundantly.

The word joy also could be substituted with the word enthusiasm. In Greek, the word "enthusiasm" denotes "en," which means "in," and God (the Greek word "theos"): God inside you. The work of God inside you is to fill you with joy and deliver you from sin. One deadly sin is what is known as a white lie. Having fun in our society will destroy many because the white lie is a smart tool the devil uses today in our homes, churches, and society. A lot of spiritual leaders today use this as a way to cheer up their congregations. But it makes our teaching and our sermons less important or pivotal. Jesus Christ did not bear the death of the cross so we can have fun, but he died in order that we may have eternal life.

If you hide a shirt somewhere in a garage for ten years you will find that it is tearing apart gradually till it is deteriorated. This is the work of moths. We may not see them with our naked eyes but their destruction is very severe. Therefore, in our lives, even tiny sins are destructive though we cannot see them. Those sins can lead to death or destruction. The sin of profanity, taking the name of the Lord in vain, seems harmless, but it is a giant killer of spiritual life.

Love is patient. Many people today are "snap" people. They seem to be impatient. Some of them, when they ask God for something, fail to wait or be patient for their request would happen. Some also are impatient with each other. That is why the world we live in is known as a speed world. People want the pizza to be delivered in two seconds. They want to cross the ocean and fly from the United States to Africa in three minutes. People do not want to cook anymore. They delight in fast food despite diseases that come with it. We want church services to be thirty minutes so we can go on with our lives. The past generation was more patient than ours. Therefore, they were able to create and invent all the technology we have today. With this speed age, many will be left behind. Only those who are more resourceful than we are will win the race. People have reduced their sleep from eight hours a day to four and there are those who are trying to cut their sleep hours to less than three. This race against the clock will do us severe harm.

Love also is kind. I have met many kind people in my life. Their acts of kindness came from their deep love for their fellow beings. Those people had their own problems just as we do, but they learned to climb above their circumstances. They refused to look at the shadow behind them; instead they focused ahead. Two of those people would not be uncomfortable being mentioned by name.

One of them used to be a veterinarian. Vandy was assigned to be my disciple after I had finished spiritual training at the rescue mission. Vandy came to my house twice a week to study the Bible with me. I had great moments with Vandy. He was in his late fifties or early sixties, but I was unaware of his advance in age. He was an excellent leader. My car tire kept going flat. Vandy showed up, took me to the place where they sold tires, and when I try to pay for it, Vandy pushed my money away and paid for it.

I loved Vandy very much, but sometimes I felt intimidated and inferior when he talked about his successful business as a Veterinarian and how he had the biggest house in the neighborhood. Deep inside I knew my brother Vandy did not mean to brag to me about how well he was doing because he told me he didn't understand why God had blessed him that much. I had an answer for you, brother, because you were humble.

The second person was George Sproul with whom I still maintain strong ties. George was working in health administration and he lost his job because of alcoholism. He then enrolled with me in a spiritual training program as a part of recovery. Finally, he accepted a job counseling at the rescue mission. George has deep compassion to save lives. Even after I had finished my training, I took a job at a phone company call center. Every now and then I go to see George just to chat with him. George is very wise and kind. He is not reluctant to whoever comes to him for a little help. George was the only one who will lend me money whenever I am short. His entire life he has a big heart to build up those who are weak. He has helped many break free from addiction. George is the kindest person I have ever seen.

The civil war has been over for two decades; however the SPLA movement abducted children to their movement as child soldiers. One of those kids is now a world icon in music. He is well accepted in Europe and North America. Emanuel Jal was a child when a British aid worker known as Ann Macune took him to Britain as a foster child. Mrs. Macune was the wife of one of the SPLA leaders who is now acting as Vice President of South Sudan. Mrs. Ann

Macune was a real angel of kindness. She saved children from the horror of war in Sudan.

Unfortunately, Mrs. Ann Macune was killed in a car accident on the streets of Nairobi, Kenya, while having a child in her womb. I was not fortunate enough to have seen that angel of love, but I believe I will see him one day in heaven.

There are many kind people around us and we have the opportunity to learn kindness from them. Love does not envy, as we have learned. Three things remain: faith, hope, and love, but the greatest is love. We Christians are told to love our enemies. It is a hard task, but if we need remain in the kingdom of God we must learn to love our enemies. Sometimes others try to drag us into envy by ignoring us and sometimes the devil uses their resources and wealth to create envy in us. Because Satan is a liar and the father of all liars he will try to convince you that you are inferior and less than the next person to you who is wealthy and you are not. But the Bible is so clear that love of money is the root of all evil.

Some people die and leave an inheritance behind for their children and the wealthy instead to blessing others. However, wealth breaks family bonds. Everyone becomes jealous of one another thinking others received a bigger share. So as we know that thievery is common in every society and many thefts are the result of money we are born with. Children who are given gifts envy what their brothers have.

Envy is not something we find. We are born with it. However, through the faith and love of God, our hearts change and we will be able to be content with what we have. Those find themselves out of faith because the devil is very beguiling and he will use someone else to destroy them. Maybe you are a single man and happy and you have the right perspective. He will use a married person to drag you into envy.

If it happens that you have kids the devil will use others or even you, the father, to love one child more than the others. But all the children are the same, male and female. We might play with the youngest kid most because he or she gives us so much joy, but we must be careful to give the same attention to each one. Sometimes it is hard to deal with kids. They all act differently. It is difficult to associate as much with a one-year-old because they are not easily understandable or they have a different mood. But we can show them love that will not generate a negative result. Some kids are extraverts; some are introverts. One is not better than the other, but they have different characteristics. Any kids are angels. We must be careful to answer their questions in order not to give them a twisted idea. Children are fast learners. Ideas they learn at the youngest age **119** determine their paths and choices.

Love does not boast. My definition of boasting is to claim that you are above everything. Psalm 34:2 (NIV) say, "My soul will boast in the LORD; let the afflicted hear and rejoice. Glorify the LORD with me; let us exalt his name together." We sometimes boast about great people, not because they are humble and servants to all. Jesus said. "Whoever wants to be great among you must be a servant." Truly great leaders turn out to be God-fearing servants. Jesus Christ was given a name above all because he chose to serve mankind with humility and completed the work of salvation. We Christians boast of our spiritual leaders, but above all, we should boast about the Lord because he is the only one worthy of our praise. Psalm 44:8 (NIV) reads, "In God we make our boast all day long..."

We can boast of our families who sacrifice their energy to bring us to Christ. The devil's primary target is the family. I remember when I was diagnosed with schizophrenia I did not know where to turn, but my family, especially my brother Giw, bore the burden with me. He is the only one who stood with me. I am very sorry that I caused him a lot of trouble, but he learned to be patient with me. In addition, when I arrived in Georgia, I was fortunate to have supportive friends; for example, Deng Bol, Garang Bol, Chan and Adet, and was supported by others such as Joseph Martin, Walid, and my cousin Guamaar.

Book Recommendations

100 Ways To Motivate Yourself: Change Your Life Forever
by Dr. Steve Chandler

PowerNomics: The National Plan to Empower Black America by Claud Anderson